EXCAVATION OF TRUTH
Unsung Heroes of 1857 War of Independence

EXCAVATION OF TRUTH

Unsung Heroes of 1857 War of Independence

Role of Muslims–Fanatical or Nationalist
At the
150th Anniversary of Martyrdom of "Mujahidin-e-Azadi"

K.M.S. Khan

Edited by
Khan Ahmed Adeel

KANISHKA PUBLISHERS, DISTRIBUTORS
NEW DELHI-110 002

KANISHKA PUBLISHERS, DISTRIBUTORS
4697/5-21 A, Ansari Road, Daryaganj
New Delhi-110 002
Phones : 2327 0497, 2328 8285
Fax : 011-2328 8285
e-mail: kanishka_publishing@yahoo.co.in

First Published 2007

ISBN 978-81-7391-976-3

PRINTED IN INDIA

Published by Madan Sachdeva for Kanishka Publishers, Distributors, 4697/5-21A, Ansari Road, Daryaganj, New Delhi-110 002, Typeset by Sunshine Graphics, Delhi, and Printed at Nice Printing Press, Delhi.

With Love to my Grand Daughter

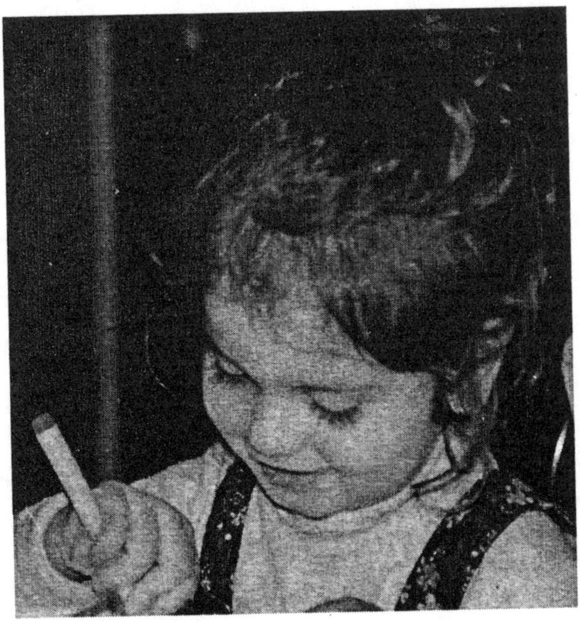

KHAN IRIS ADEEL

Tartari by Mother's blood, Afghani by Father's blood, Mangolian by Grand Mother's blood, Indian by heredity and Azri by Birth.

Prof. S.M. Azizuddin Husain
Director

JAMIA MILLIA ISLAMIA

Jamia's Premchand Archives and Literary Centre
Maulana Mohammed Ali Jauhar Marg, New Delhi-25

Foreword

I feel the pleasure in writing foreword for the book *Excavation of Truth: Unsung Heroes of 1857 War of Independence.* The British called it a revolt, mutiny, amongst other things. Sir Saiyid Ahmed Khan wrote two books on the subject—*Sarkashi-i-Zila Bijnor* in 1858 and *Asbab-i-Bhaghawat-i-Hind* in 1859. After this we slept on this topic and gave the space to the British and other colonial historians to write whatever they liked on 1857. In National Archives of India, New Delhi and Bhopal, more than 30,000 documents in Persian and Urdu are waiting for attention of the historians. In U.P. State Archives. Lucknow and Allahabad, thousands of documents are lying without being consulted till now. These documents contain a wealth of information on situation in the major centers of revolt in U.P. like, Muradabad, Aligarh, Lucknow, etc. Same has been the case of Bihar State Archives, Patna. I congratulate Mr. K.M.S. Khan on his efforts to introduce us with the role of Maulvi Peer Ali Khan in the first war of independence. Whether one agrees or disagrees with the thesis of Mr. Khan is a different issue, but what is important is that the has thrown light on an important aspect of 1857 which has hitherto been neglected by the others.

I am sure that scholars working on 1857 would find this work very useful in their researches.

29th March, 2007 **Prof. S.M. Azizuddin Husain**

Contents

An Opinion

I, being one of the few privileged persons who were provided the advance copy of the manuscript for suggestions. After going through the manuscript two/ three times, instead giving suggestions I prefer to give my opinion/ observations.

"Excavation of Truth" is an invaluable effort to uncover the Historical truth, which hitherto had remained buried for the last over 150 years due to political and religious prejudices. Author's thrust on the glorious role of Muslims out of common men to save Indian sub-continent from being enslaved by Europeans, more particularly by Britishers gives us a source to be proud of our past. "Peer Ali Khan" an unsung Martyr of 1857, hailing from my father's native place has made us proud of our heredity. But I am also sad that such brave, selfless patriots were ignored and were deprived of their due honour. They struggled and sacrificed their life for the honour of the "Watan".

I found the book structured on the strong pillars of facts and depicts great combination of struggle, intelligence, patriotism, bravery and extreme sacrifices of Muslims for the freedom of the Indian sub-continent.

The author has rightly condemned those who malafidely call these "Mujahideen" as "Traitors" or "Terrorist" who proved their loyalty to the Motherland. I find this piece of work, an extraordinary effort for all discerning people not only of India but of entire South Asia, a source of enlightenment.

Araish Azfar

March, 2007

Visiting Lecturer: Govt. Degree
Science and Commerce College –Karachi
A/462 Block-J, North Nazimabad
KARACHI

Preface

(What Inspired Me to Write this Book)

"Fighter's of Freedom" a book in English was prescribed by U.P. Board of Secondary Education in 50's for 7th standard. I was at that time student of Shibli National Inter College Azamgarh, U.P. India. What disturbed me most in the said book that out of about a dozen personalities mentioned therein as fighters of freedom, only one Muslim (Maulana Abbul Kalam Azad) and rest were Hindus. Even at that stage when I was about 10 years of age, I felt ashamed that Muslims did not do anything for the Independence of the Country, and did not participate in the freedom Movement. That was the period just after the partition of India and Muslim Community was being accused for the Partition and generally were being asked to migrate to Pakistan or Qabristan (Graveyard). The feeling of hatred which should have been against the Britishers who enslaved India for almost 200 years and unleashed all sorts of cruelty and savagery over the Indians, was systematically diverted towards the Muslims. It was the period of great demoralisation for Muslims of India, and I was one of them, though not matured enough to understand the politics, but the Sarcasm of Hindu friends was really hurting.

Whenever I used to express my hurt feelings to my uncle late Maqbool Ahmad Khan a cousin of my father, he used to tell me that all is wrong and malicious propaganda. Lacs of Muslims throughout India, including from my own village Mohammadpur District Azamgarh, U.P. India sacrificed their lives for the independence of the Country. But except his words I could not find their names anywhere in any of the textbooks to which at that stage I could lay my hand.

While I was in B.Com Final in 1959/60 my father who was confined to bed for the last over two years expired, which brought responsibilities of the family on my shoulders. In August, 1960 after completing my graduation from Shibli Post Graduate College, Azamgarh I had to leave my further studies and went Bombay looking for a job. Since 1960 to 1963 I had virtually sidelined those grim feelings which kept me bothering during my school days due to lack of time to think anything else except concentrating on my career to achieve a respectable living and support my family. However, in 1962 when China attacked India and suddenly in 1963 many prominent Muslims, which included late Mehboob R. Khan the film Producer (Mother India and Son of India etc.) and Yousuf Khan popularly known as Dilip Kumar were accused as Anti-national and their houses and business premises were raided. Since I was working with late Mehboob Khan and knew them too well, and knew that there could not have been a bigger slanderous allegation to call them as anti-national.

Immediately thereafter I started my search of "Truth" about the Role of Muslims of Indian Nationalism. Here a friend late Shyam Sunder, "Munnawar" who was the Editor of a Weekly magazine, "Chitra Weekly" helped me to get the membership of Hardayal Municipal Library—near Old Delhi Railway Station, Delhi. I started spending 2/3 hours, twice/thrice in a week reading books of the Medieval period and thereafter upto the independence of the Country. Side by side I started looking to any book and articles which dealt with the Independence Movement of 1857, which developed in me the interest in the History. The more I got involved into the research the more I got enlightened about the truth and found that the tirade unleashed against Muslims of India being projected as non-nationalist or anti-national is absolutely false and malicious propaganda. Muslims of India irrespective, whether their fore-fathers were, Turks, Afghans, Arabs or Mangolian became Indianised and sacrificed their lives and wealth for the honour of this Country India. The accusation attributed to them as anti-National or non-nationalist is nothing but false propaganda. Even the partition of the country is not because of Muslims but was the result of shortsighted policies of the then leaders including Indian National Congress and Muslims league.

The Urdu poet Anwar Hussain Anwar has rightly said:

"Taqseem-Men zameen ki sab ka hath tha,
(In the partition of the land (India) everybody was involved)

Ilzaam sare mere buzargon pe rakh dia."
(But the entire blame was foisted upon my ancestors)

I have tried to analyse from the records of 1857 written by those who were contemporary of those events which took place during 1857. The contents of the book are based on the true historical facts. The objective is to highlight the crucial role played by the Muslims, in sacrificing their lives for the motherland "INDIA" without any selfish motive in their act of aggressiveness towards the common enemy. In order to understand these facts one has to go through the contents carefully with patience and open mind.

Why the role of Muslims were not brought into limelight, was it our own brothers to create this distance or was it another dice thrown by the Colonial Empire in their efforts of divide and rule policy, which is being felt even today?

March, 2007 **Khan Mohd. Sadiq Khan**

Acknowledgements

My special thanks to "Al-Mighty" Allah, for providing me the vision to venture on this project as a homage to the Martyrs, forgotten by the people of this Country.

I pay my respect and thanks to:

(a) My late father Abdul Hadi Khan who inculcated in me the strength to call a spade a shade. He developed in me the self-respect and self-confidence as even in my teens he used to seek my opinion on various domestic affairs and gave respect to my views.

(b) My late mother, Mehrun Nisa Khanam who inculcated in me the strength to speak the truth without fear, as Allah helps those who speak the truth.

(c) My late elder brother Mohd. Hadi Khan about 9 years elder to me and died at the prime of his youth. He was my Role Model as I found him ever ready to help the needy in whatever way he could without any expectation in return. I am privileged that it was he who got me admitted in the School and my admission form is in his handwriting.

(d) My late 'Chacha' Hafiz Abdul Ghani Khan, who stood like a rock and never let us feel the loss of our father.

(e) My uncle late Maqbool Ahmad Khan a maternal cousin of my father, a born genius, who is the main source and inspiration to me to write the History of my village Mohammadpur and the Shaheed Watan Maulvi Peer Ali Khan.

I pray to Allah to provide all of them and my other elders a special space with all the privileges in the most sacred Heaven. Ameen.

My thanks to Mr. Kropf Mario who is responsible to provide me the break-through on the execution of Peer Ali Khan by William Taylor out of the Taylor's book, "Patna Crisis—Three Months at Patna" and the books of A.K. Biswas and Prof. I.K. Shukla's "Unsung Martyrs of 1857". Mr. Mario, a Swis National is the Managing Director of Panal Pina Central Asia in BAKU—Azarbaijan.

I congratulate my son Khan Ahmed Adeel in not only showing keen interest in the compilation of the book's manuscript but actively participating in the process of browsing the material and editing. Thank you *bete.*

My thanks to Mohd. Haseen Khan, grand son of late Maqbool Ahmad Khan, resident of Los Angles—U.S. A. in providing me the book "A History of Indian Mutiny" by T.R.E. Holmes.

My thanks to one Mr. Roshanlal who gifted me the book, "The War of Independence, 1857-59" containing the letters of Carl Marx written from India in 1857, and published in New York Tribune.

My love and thanks to my daughter Khan Tazien for designing the cover page.

I also express my gratitude to Mr. Naved Saheb of "Hamdard Trust Karachi" in providing me the book Brani's "History of Tughlaks"—English translation by S. Moinul Haque and to Mr. Hammad of "Hamdard Trust", New Delhi.

And to my wife Sarwat S. Khan, my special gratitude to her for creating a congenial atmosphere in the house which allowed me to work on this project peacefully and with full concentration.

My thanks to Dr. Imtiaz Ahmad, Director, Khuda Baksh Oriental Public Library—Patna for the co-operation.

I must express my regrets on the indifferent and non co-operative attitude of:

(a) Bihar State Archives—Patna.

(b) Regional Archives Office—Allahabad.

(c) Archeological Survey of India—Sarnath–Varanasi.

(d) Asiatic Society—Calcutta.

(e) Raza Library—Rampur.

Who did not even bother to reply to any of my letters sent by e-mail and registered/speed post. As against that my thanks to Foreign Libraries and publishers who all responded promptly to my letters.

In the end I will be failing in my moral duty if I do not acknowledge the help I received from Meena, the little girl who without frown rather with sincerity got the manuscript ready which would have been, if not impossible, very difficult to complete. Thank you, Meena, God bless you and your family. Aameen.

March, 2007 **Khan Mohd. Sadiq Khan**

"BIS MILLAH-HIR-REHMANIR-RAHEEM"

1

Introduction and Main Objective of the Book

India became independent on 15th August, 1947, has also celebrated "Golden Jubilee" of Independence in 1997. It is 2007, and India is celebrating 150th Anniversary of 1st Independence movement of 1857. However, the sacrifices of Muslims for the Independence of the "Watan-e-Azeem" Hindustan has been systematically erased rather buried in the confines of the Archives. The historians systematically ignored them. Why is the big question? On top of it, all through, the Muslims have been and are being shown in the negative and in bad light on the question of nationalism. As for the British historians are concerned they had the reason, because they were opposed by the Muslims in their design of enslaving India. But the role of Indian historians put them in the Dock? I have tried to analyze it here for the future generation.

It is generally, made to believe that the movement for independence of the country started in 1857. Mangal Pandey is considered as the originator of the movement. However, the trial record of Mangal Pandey shows a different picture. His revolt was not on account of Patriotism, but purely on religious grounds. Be that, as it may, the fact is that the Independence movement started much before 1857 and by the Muslims of the Country.

In about 15th and 16th centuries AD when Portuguese and then French came to India and made efforts to convert the Locals both Hindus and Muslims, mostly deprived classes to Christianity, and for this purpose they used both lurements and force. The

Moghal rulers at that time did not have full control of Southern India, ruled by small time Rajas who were not strong enough or were not bothered about the plights of common men hence the people were left to defend themselves. The Muslim Ulema of Kerala resisted and tried their best to throw them out of the Indian Soil. Later Britishers came in the country. For sometimes, they got involved with French to gain the supremacy over each other. During this period there was some relief to the local populace.

The Britishers after confining French and Portuguese in Pondicherry and Goa etc., and after purchasing Bombay from a Hindu Raja turned their attention to Eastern part of India and established themselves 1st as trader then started spreading their activities to achieve their ultimate goal to enslave India.

In 1658 AD, the then Subedar of Bengal Shaista Khan found the activities of Britishers much more than mere trading. The Britishers wanted to dislodge the local peasants from their cultivable land and grab it. The Nawab challenged the Britishers. The Britishers started fortifying their Trade Centres and simultaneously they started employing local ruffians and training them in Arms. This news was reported to the then Moghal King, Aurangzeb who immediately instructed all his Governors (Subedars) to close all the British Trade Centres and confiscate all the goods of Britishers and arrest them. Most of the Britishers ran away, and took refuge outside the domane of Moghal Empire, and made 3 attempts with their war (Beras) ships at Chatagang, but were repulsed. Having failed on this front they started marine robberies specially to Haj Pilgrims and Arab traders.

When Britishers failed in their policy of pressure of force and rowdism they adopted the last resort of (Khushamad) i.e. shoelicking of the king and sought pardon from Aurangzeb. This they did through Ibrahim Khan who replaced Shaista Khan as Viceroy (Governor) of Bengal. Ibrahim Khan was very friendly with Britishers hence Britishers used him to achieve their object.

(Ref. Tehreeke-Azadi-Men Ulema ka Kirdar" by Faisal Ahmed Bhat Kali Nadvi—Publisher; Majlise Tehqeeqat Wa Nashriat Islam Lucknow).

According to Sir Jadav Nath Sarkar in his book the "History of Aurangzeb", Vol-V, p. 252:

> "We turn to the action of Imperial Court during 1687-89. The sack of Hughli (28th October 1686) and the seizure of Hijli (February, 1687) by the English had been reported to Aurangzeb, then engaged in the siege of Golkonda. The next provocation by the English had been the attack on his shipping in the Western Sea by the Bombay fleet (under direction of Sir John Child).
>
> The Emperor had immediately ordered the arrest of all the Englishmen, the occupation of their factories all over his dominion, and the prohibition of all trade or other intercourse with the audacious foreigners by his subjects."

Here Sir Jadav Nath Sarkar expresses his opinion that because the Britishers were "supreme" at Sea and could stop the journey of pilgrimships to Mecca and also loss of revenue which was coming from the British trading forced Aurangzeb to make settlement with Britishers cannot be accepted as true because Aurangzeb never compromised on his principle on material considerations.

Aurangzeb died in 1707. Subsequent Moghal rulers being incompetent, gave the Britishers an open field to establish themselves and dislodge local Nawabs and Rajas from their rule one after the other. They also started making home in the minds of Hindu population that if Hindus will support Britishers they will give Hindus their own Raj by dislodging Muslims who have been ruling them for many centuries. Hindus did not realize the Britishers game plan of creating wedge between Hindus and Muslims, so as to enslave India ultimately.

After the death of Aurangzeb not one Moghal ruler was competent or strong enough to defend their kingdom, hence the Imperial Kingdom of Moghal Empire shattered in pieces and many incompetent, greedy Nawabs and Rajas numbering over 250 small states came into being. Only two out of them were comparatively stronger States viz. Oudh and Bengal.

After about 49 years of the death of Aurangzeb, Nawab Ali Wardi Khan the ruler of Bengal followed by his successor Nawab Sirajuddaula tried to throw the Britishers out of the country. This was 3rd attempt by Indians specially Muslims against Europeans. First attempt was made in 15th century AD by Kerala Muslims/ Ulema over 300 years before 1857, followed by Aurangzeb in 1668 AD and by Sirajuddaula in 1756 and then by Hyder Ali in 1767 followed by his son Teepu Sultan till 1799.

While crowning Sirajuddaula as ruler of Bengal his Uncle (*Chacha*) Nawab Ali Wardi Khan cautioned Sirajuddaula to be watchful of the activities of Britishers. Sirajuddaula after assuming power, found the activities of Britishers against the interest of the State hence he started striving to check and restrict their activities. Robert Clive did not relish the check by Sirajuddaula hence on 13.06.1756 he along with 1000 Europeans and 2000 Indian soldiers assembled in Mushidabad against Sirajuddaula, but was defeated by Sirajuddaula on 21.06.1756. Robert Clive then purchased the Deevans of Sirajuddaula Rai Vallabh Rai and Jagat Seth Mehtab Rai through the Calcutta's Richest businessman Seth Ami Chand. Clive also took Mir Jaffar the son-in-law of Nawab Ali Wardi to his side, with lurement to make him Nawab. Mir Jaffar gave a big price for the same in cash to Clive which Clive had committed to pay to Seth Ami Chand. Accordingly, on 23rd June, 1757 in the war at Pilasi, Sirajuddaula was defeated and was killed on 2nd July, 1757 by one Mohd. Beg, a Ghaddare Watan. Here the British were helped and supported by the Nawab of Karnataka, the two Dewans of Sirajuddaula, Rai Vallabh Rai and Jagat Seth Mehtab Rai and Mir Jaffar and Seth Ami Chand who were purchased by Britishers and conspired against Sirajuddaula during the War. Thus Britishers established their full control over Bengal and placed the greedy Mir Jaffer as the Bengal's ruler. Later Qasim Ali, son-in-law of Mir Jaffar repaid the Traitor Mir Jafar in the same coin and conspired against his father-in-law with the Britishers and got himself replaced as the ruler of Bengal. In December, 1763/1764 Britishers removed Qasim Ali from Bengal and re-installed Mir Jaffar in his place. Thereafter Britishers took over the full control of Bengal as independent rulers. If Sirajuddaula would have got support from Hindu rulers such as

Marathas, Sindias and Rajputs India would have been cleaned of Britishers hundred years before 1857 and 190 years before 1947.

After Bengal the Britishers directed their force to South India. There too only a Muslim, Hyder Ali followed by his son Teepu Sultan had challenged the Britishers and continued their fight for over 32 long years till 1799 when Teepu attained the Martyrdom. Here too the same story of treachery by few Maulvis, Pandits and Mir Sadiq. Peshwa and Nizam had joined and signed the treaty with British on 4th July, 1789 and with their support Britishers established their control over South India also. Punjab province has been staunch ally of British in Northern India. Thus Bengal in Eastern India, Madras in Southern India and Punjab the Western/Northern India plus the Allies of British, such as Nizam, Marathas, Sindias, various Rajas of Punjab and Rajputana and Banaras in Oudh became the regions in direct control of British by 1800 A.D.

Next sixty years Britishers created hell for the people of Oudh and Delhi through its Residents who were virtually ruling Delhi as well as Oudh, in the name of Nawab and the King. Bahadur Shah Zafar was virtually an invalid King. Wajid Ali Shah the Nawab of Oudh was deposed on 04.02.1856 arrested and shifted to Calcutta and placed in House arrest in "Matia Burj". Later on 05.07.1856 the minor son of Wajid Ali Shah, Birjisqadar was named as the Nawab and Begum Hazrat Mahal as guardian under the Salarship of one Mamoo Khan. Subsequently when the Britishers wanted to takeover the Oudh completely the Begum resisted bravely and not finding any help shifted to Sitapur side and there too resisted for sometimes but found no help from any side by any other Raja or Nawab, ultimately, with all her dependents went in exile in the hills of Nepal but did not surrender. Nana Rao and Tantia Tope also went to Nepal alongwith Begum Hazrat Mahal.

The Begum Hazrat Mahal was described by T.R.E. Homes in his book "A History of Indian Mutiny", p. 523:

> "The leader of the kings sepoys was the Begum who in spirit and ability, was rival of the Rani of Jhansi."

G.W. Forrest in his book "A History of Indian Mutiny" 3rd Vol., p. 484 narrating the action at Nawabganj at Faizabad Road describes the Begum Hazrat Mahal as "Most Formidable of the Rebel Leaders, the Begum":

> "From Baree, Hope Grant turned to right and proceeded north to Muhammadabad, close to the 'Gagra' in the expectation of intercepting the 'most formidable' of the rebel leaders, the Begum."

Columnist Hamid Husain in an article, "The Story of the Storms, 1857" looks at the 1857 War of Independence dispassionately based on the works of:

Ward, Andrew—Our Bones, pp. 63-64.
Collier, Richard—The Great Indian Mutiny, p. 234.
Choudhry, Shashi—Civil Rebellion, pp. 132-34 and 143.

Describes Beghum Hazrat Mahal:

> "The former dancing girl and later the Queen Hazrat Mahal's behaviour was more praiseworthy than her debauch husband, Wajid Ali Shah. Wajid when told about his exile was 'weeping, pleading, baring his head to the appalled and embarrassed Colonel Outram. On the contrary, in November when a shell hit the palace gate, the garrison panicked and soldiers fled away. The indomitable Hazrat Mahal remained staunch and when told chiefs to cut her head before running away, they stayed feeling the shame and humiliation. On another occasion, she sent a pair of women's trousers to a faint-hearted chief with a note stating that better he should put them on and to retire to his proper place—a harem. She spent 50,000 sterling pounds of her own money to build a wall around the city. She had the rare leadership qualities to gain the confidence of both Hindus and Muslims. She was able to prevent the division between two communities due to the activities of religious zealots like Maulvi Massih-us-Zaman and Babar Ali. In this effort, she was helped by Maulvi Ahmadullah Shah, who not only worked for cooperation between Hindus and Muslims but between Shias and Sunnis of Lucknow. She was able to rally the soldiers, landed nobility and city population to her cause.

> In middle of 1859, when the rebel cause seemed to be doomed, Hazrat Mahal and her two staunch Hindu allies, Beni Madho and Hanumant Singh refused to surrender to British."

Karl Marx, pp. 197-98 in the book, "The First War of Independence" mentions:

> "During July-August-September, 1858 Begum made the final attempt but failed and moved across the Rapti River alongwith Nana Rao, to the territory of English Dog man, Jangbahadur of Nepal, and settled into the Hills of Nepal. Nana Rao is supposed to have died in Nepal."

Another supporter of Begum Hazrat Mahal Beghum Alia in fact acted as a full-fledged General and commanded the Sepoys. But these Sepoys were mostly those who had escaped from Delhi's Kingdom and were cowards and ran away from the battle field, still these Ladies did not surrender.

This shows the brave resistance shown even by Muslim Ladies. Here too the Wazeer-e-Azam of Awadh Mir Ali Naqi conspired with Britishers against the Begum Hazrat Mahal.

Some of the Kings, Rajas and Generals (other than brave men from common people) who fought against the Britishers are, General Bakht Khan, General Mehmood Khan, Khan Bahadur Khan, Tantia Tope, Shehzada Firoz Shah a nephew of Bahadur Shah Zafar and the brave Maharani Lakshmi Bai (*Jhansi Ki Rani*), Nana Rao, and Babu Kunwar Singh. (Ref. p. 276, Bagi-e-Hindustan).

Karl Marx further noted between, pp. 188-98 regarding following as under:

Man Singh:	" An Indian Raja. In August 1858 joined the rebels, but early, 1859 betrayed the well-known leader of the uprising, Tantia Tope."
Man Singh of Oudh	Big feudal land owner of Oudh Kingdom, was an ally of English Colonialists, during National Liberation uprising of 1857-1859."

(Contd.)

Tantia Tope:	A cousin of Nana Rao, born in 1812 and executed in 1859 was a gifted Maratha General and leader of National liberation uprising of 1857-59 in India headed rebel detachment, in Cawnpore- Kalpi and Gwalier areas in 1859 was betrayed and was executed after being detected in his hiding place in Nepal in 1859 early. The Betrayal was done by Raja Man Singh.
Ranbeer Singh	"Raja of Kashmeer, acted on the side of the English during National Liberation uprising of 1857-1859."
Sindhia Aalijah (Jiyaji Bhagirath Rao)	"Maratha Prince of Gwaliar, Principality, during the National liberation uprising of 1857-59, in 1835, sided with English."

The subject matter of this book is not the Nawabs or Jagirdars. There engagements, if at all, there was any, with Britishers may have been to save their power and the territory or grudge of denial of the Pension which their adopted fathers and/ or husbands were getting from Britisher such as Nana Rao, Jhansi Ki Rani and some others. Their fight was not on National considerations. Here I am concerned with those brave and selfless Muslims from common men who fought and sacrificed their life purely for the independence of this country or to put it, to save India from being enslaved by Britishers. They were not given due place in the History. Their sacrifices were systematically covered under thick layers of Archives thus gave opportunity to vested interest to spread falsehood. They were and even now are named with various derogatory names, such as, fanatics, disloyal, fundamentalist, bigotry, terrorists, mendicant, rebellious and hereditary disloyal. These are the titles given and used by British to the Muslims and Indian Media, print or electronic highlight it and show their contempt against Muslims as a whole.

The Sepoy Movement from Meerut on 24.04.1857 was given the colour of Mutiny by Britishers and by Indian historians as the 1st Independent movement. By Britishers as an excuse to unleash cruelty and by Indian historians to cover the truth, because actual independence movement was by Muslims only. The Hindus were loyal to Britishers. The native Sepoys in British army included

Hindus and Muslims but their revolt was on religious ground and not on National considerations. I quote here the words of Mr. Gautam Jetly, Publisher: Asian Educational Service, New Delhi.

"It is not easy to unravel the cause of Mutiny". But was it an uprising against oppression, or, a movement to fulfill a prophecy? The very start of the Mutiny finishes the debate of whether the uprising was national in nature?

The fall out of this movement saw the seventy kilometer stretch from Meerut to Delhi only Muslims, were picked up and hanged on trees and left hanging for days together to create terror. Practically all the British historians and writers such as, T.R.E. Holmes, G.W.Forrest, William Taylor, Humphry, Charles Allen and his great grandfather George Allen, W. Hunter, G.B. Malleson J.Kaye, and many other British stated in their books and memoirs etc. that those revolted were shouting the slogan of "Deen-Deen" Ali-Ali "Nara-e-Takbeer" and "Allah-o-Akbar". This is proof enough to show that it were only Muslims and no other Community which revolted against Britishers.

Group of Muslim Ulema, known and described by Britishers as "Wahabee" Sect were actively preaching against the Britishers as they found that the activities of Britishers, were destroying the very fabric of Islamic as well as Indian culture. With the result in 1857 only in Bihar and Oudh over 50 thousand Ulema were hanged by Britishers without any trial. Another active group of Ulema other than so-called Wahabees, who undertook Jehad against Britishers are detailed in the book "Tehreek-e-Azadi Men Ulema Ka Kirdar" by Faisal Ahmed Bhat Kali Nadvi, published by Majlise Tehqeeqat Wa Nashriat Islam Lucknow, 1st Ed. June, 2003. Besides the above "Tareekh Ajeeb" and "Kala Pani" by Maulvi Jafar Thanesari available in "Lutan Library" of Andman and Nikobar Island gives the details of Ulema exiled to Andaman and Nikobar Island (p. 229, Baghi-e-Hindustan).

In the book "Tehreek-e-Azadi Men Ulema Ka Kirdar", p. 52 from the book "Humphry's Memoirs", at p. 12 quoted, Humphry (an Agent of British secret Service and was in the employment of East India Company Government) expressed his feelings of uneasiness:

"Muslim Ulema were also cause of our concern. They were too biased against Britishers and were not ready to budge even an inch out of their conception. Kings and Umra included all were small in the presence of Ulema."

At page 218 of Chaturbhuj's "Memoirs of William Taylor" and William Taylor's "Thirty Eight years in India", Vol-II, p. 240 is quoted from "Red Pamphlet" of Calcutta:

"It may be easily imagined that with a rebellion incited, fostered, and kept up by Mohammedans, a city in which men of that religion formed a preponderating class, must be an object of no ordinary anxiety. From the day of Meer Kasim Ali, Patna had always been a rebellious city. Even so lately as 1846, the Mohammedan nobility had endeavoured to take advantage of our balanced fortunes on the bank of the Sutluj."

The above and many more quotes of Britishers show as to who were actually involved in the revolt against the British and how much they were afraid of Mohammedans.

Among the Muslims who voluntarily joined the Rebellion, under the impulse of joining a righteous war, or jehad so were called mujahids or jihadis, but the British termed them as "fanatics".

The Muslims out of common men were involved in the movement purely on National consideration. Unfortunately, there was no Joint Movement. It was sort of regional movement by individuals.

Charles Allen an Indian born British writer/historian in his latest book "God's Terrorist" published from London by Little Brown in February' 2006, p. 125 writes:

"In Patna, Lucknow, Delhi and elsewhere group of idealists sought the over throw of the company Raj and exchanged cautiously worded correspondence."

"Had these various conspirators acted together, the outcome of the 1857 Mutiny would have been very different."

Dr. Motichand the then Director, Prince of Wales Museum Bombay in his book, "Kashi Ka Itihas" 1st Edition dated September', 1962, p. 3 also expressed the above opinion:

> "At the end of 18th century and middle of 19th century, the 1857 revolt is an important incidence, but its effect was local and not of National nature."

Maulvi Peer Ali Khan was leader in Patna (Azeemabad) Division. Peer Ali Khan was in the group of Maulvi Massih-us-Zaman and Maulvi Ahmadullah Madrasi of Oudh Lucknow as was revealed from the letters and papers captured from his shop after his hanging. Maulvi Liyaqat Ali leader in Allahabad Region, Maulvi Shah Ahmadullah Madrasi in Oudh and Rohel Khand Regions, Shaheed Saiyed Ahmad and Saiyed Amir in Peshawar region, Maulvi Naseemullah in Aligarh. Then there were supporters in villages to these leaders. They individually, organized and challenged the Britishers, and spear headed the movement for Independence. Maulvi Peer Ali Khan was hanged on 7th July, 1857 in Patna. Maulvi Shah Ahmadullah Madrasi was treacherously killed on 5th June, 1858 (15th June, 1858 in Bhaghi-e-Hindustan) by Raja of Pawayan Balwant Singh an ally of Britishers in Rohel Khand Division. Balwant Singh then to please the British presented the head of Maulvi Ahmadullah to the British Commission in Shahjahanpur, who got it hanged at the Kotwali. Later his head was buried in Daryapur Mohallah of Jahanabad, Muttasil (near) Ahmadpura, by the side of the Masjid, in Shahjahanpur, (p. 216, Baghi-e-Hindustan). Karl Marx's book, p. 237 describes Maulvi Ahmadullah Madrasi:

> "A prominent leader of the National liberation uprising of 1857-59 in India. Spokesman for the people's interest, led a rebellion in Oudh bravely, and stood at the head of the defence of Lucknow, treacherously killed in June, 1858."

Saiyed Amir was described by Britishers a "MENDICANT FANATIC" (means a person living on beggary). *(Ref. p. 364, A History of Indian Mutiny by T.R.E. Holmes)*. This shows the height of hatred by Britishers against Muslims because they opposed them in their design. Maulvi Liyaqat Ali was arrested, tried and sent for rest of his life to Andaman and Nikobar's Island known as Ross Island, "Namak-Bhatha" South point, where he died and is buried by the side of the grave of another Mujahide Azaadi Allama Fazle Haque Khairabadi (Distt: Sitapur) who was also sentenced as Baghi-e-Hindustan. The Island is considered as the worst place for human habitation creating worst type of skin disease. (Ref. Book Baghi-e-Hindustan, pp. 77, 79 and 440). All the above brave men and many more Muslims were spear-heading individually in their region and made the Britishers at the verge of flight but because of no co-ordination among them and non-support from Hindu population failed and attained "Shahadat" and the country became the slave. All the above and many more faced the extreme torture and then were hanged. But all of them accepted the death "Unbowed" and no one craved pardon.

Baghi-e-Hindustan, p. 213 mentions that Maulvi Ahmadullah Madrasi had virtually captured Lucknow and was virtual ruler prior to the installation of minor son of Wajid Ali Shah on 05.07.1857. He had adopted the title of "Shah Dilaverjung" and was called "Maulvi Ahmadullah Shah Dilaverjung Madrasi."

Great sacrifices of Muslims for independence of the country are systematically buried and allowed to be forgotten.

This gave the vested interests of the country an open field to propagate and start tirade against Muslims. Those supported the Britishers to establish their empire and enslave India claim themselves as Patriots and Nationalist and those whose blood is mixed in every inch of the country's earth are being projected as traitors and anti-national. What a Pity?

Even today because some Muslims refused to sing a song described National Geet "Vande Matram" Muslims are asked to leave the country as if the country belongs to them only, who prefer to sing the said song even if their activities may be against the interest of the Nation. Great Ravindra Nath Tagore described the said song in his letter written in 1937 (70 years before) to the Greatest Subhash Chandra Bose as under:

"The core of Vande Matram is a hymn to goddess Durga: this is so plain that there can be no debate about it. Of course, Bankim does show Durga to be inseparably united with Bengal in the end, but no Mussalman (Muslim) can be expected patriotically to worship the ten-handed deity as Swadesh."

Ref.: *Hindustan Times*, daily New Delhi dated 30.08.2006.

Such elements are well answered by the Urdu Poet Qais Rampuri:

"HAMAIN KYA DHAMKIYAN DETE HAIN SEWAK SANGHI
(How can the leaders of Sewak Sanghi threaten us)
KE REHBAR

KHUDA KA SHUKR HAI ANGREZ KE MUKHBIR NA
(Thank God we were not the informers of Britishers)
THE HUM

HAQEEQAT HAI KI ZANJEERE GHULAMI HUM NE
(It is a fact that the manacle of slavery was snapped by us)
KATEE HAI

KABHEE NAZRE SALASIL THEY KABHI SOOLEE NASHIN
(We were either thorn in their eyes or object of gallows)
THE HUM"

But again I must blame our Muslim historians who are more responsible to forget and burry the truth. Here it will not be out of place to quote Allama Iqbal (B. 1873-D, 1943):

"*ek qaum ya ek millat ki zindagi mein tareekh ki zabardastt ahmiyat hai* (History has great importance in the life of any race or nation)–*kyon ki agar uski tareekh gum ho jai ya gumnamee ki motee tahon ke neeche dafan ho jae* (because if its History is lost or buried in the thick layers of ignorance)–*to us qaum ki zindagee bhee be manee ho kar reh jatee hai?* (then the life and spirit of such race and nation becomes irrelevant") (*Rashtrya Sahara,* Urdu, Delhi Edition, dated 14.08.2005 an article by Engineer Khursheed Ghani of Asan Sole-2-Bihar).

Yes, because we the Muslims of India as a Qaum and Millat have allowed, the true History and sacrifices of Muslims for the country, burry under the thick layers of "Gumnamee", that is why we the Muslims in India are being treated shabbily in the National Stream and are falsely accused as Anti-National and their existence in the National stream is being tried to be projected as irrelevant.

My self-respect forced me to find-out the truth. If the Muslims of India are really anti-national? Or the Muslims of India have done nothing for the independence of the Country?

The truth about the sacrifices of Muslims in the National Movement is not allowed to come out and the falsehood to discredit Muslims is prominently published by all the leading English and Hindi News Papers including electronic Media.

The latest example is the book, "God's Terrorist" by Charles Allen an India born Britisher born in Kanpur. He has tried to project "Saiyed Ahmad Shaheed" as terrorist, who faught with Britishers in 1857 from Bengal to Peshawar and upto Madras and wanted to throw them out of Indian Soil. His object of Jehad against Britishers has been described by Professor Khaleeq Ahmad Nizam in his book "Hazrat Saiyed Ahmad Shaheed Aur Unke Tehreek-e-Istiqbal Wa Jehad", p. 28:

> "The very object of Saiyed Sahebs movement was to finish the British Occupation and power from Indian Soil because both Hindus and Muslims were the sufferers. Because of this reason Saiyed Saheb invited Hindus also to join in his strife to remove Britishers from Indian Soil. He told both Hindus and Muslims that, they will join him with clear and only object to free India from the Foreign rule. Thereafter who will rule the country (Hindu or Muslim) you should not bother. Whosoever (Hindus or Muslims) will be capable to rule will rule. May be both."

A person with such clear Nationalist character has been projected by Shevlin Sebastian, (*Hindustan Times,* New Delhi issue dated 19.11.2006, p. 14) based on Charles Allen's "God's Terrorists" as "Saiyed Ahmad was India's Osama." This heading in bold letters in *Hindustan Times* is inspite of the fact that inside the article the writer himself quotes Charles Allen, that "My book is a work in progress and, I have been drawing only on British sources. Problem is that I cannot speak Urdu and therefore cannot access Urdu Work." Still Shevlin Sebastian passed his judgement and branded him Terrorist of 18th century and our Indian daily gives it a bold headline.

The biased attitude of media is also clear from the letter to the Editor of one, Sahebzada Sagheer Ahmad, a retired Government Officer R/o 4/351, Noor Bagh, Ameer-e-Nishan, Aligarh published in Urdu, Newspaper, *Qaumi Awaz,* New Delhi issue dated 24.01.2007. He writes:

> "In 1953, I was appointed administrator to the "Amawasia mela" in Chitrakoot, because at the time I was studying *Holy Geeta and Holy Ramayana* and was aware about the activities in the *Mela.* Shri Jagan Prashad Rawat, the then Home Minister, Government of U.P., the Editors of English Daily 'Amrit Bazar Patrika', and 'The Leader' as well as Hindi Daily 'Bharat' alongwith the Director Information Government of Uttar Pradesh were also present in Chitrakoot. All the above persons, and myself were staying in the famous *Dharam Shala of Chitrakoot.* In the same *Dharam Shala*, Mr. Hanuman Prashad Poddar, Editor Monthly 'Kalleyan', Shri Prabhu Dut Braham Charji, and famous religious Guru, Tojenya Mahatma Kirpatriji and a retired Judge, Chandrabhal Misra, were all staying.
>
> The *Mahant* of the Chitrakoot's 'Balaji Temple' in the course of discussion showed me the 'Tampatra' on Bras Plate, of the size 4½' × 3' containing the Farman of Moghal King Aurangzeb plus the papers granting some villages by Aurangzeb for construction and upkeep of the 'Balaji Mandir'. I invited all the above persons including the Editors of all the newspapers as well weekly. They all were astonished to see the papers and the 'Tampatra', because all along they considered Aurangzeb a Temple breaker, and it was a shock to them that Aurangzeb could be the builder of Temple? All the people and the Editors noted the details.

After returning to Allahabad I started collecting all the daily news papers for months together whose editors were in Chitrakoot and had noted the details of Aurangzeb's Farmans. The visit of Chitrakoot by the Editors and details of *Mela* were published but none of them wrote even a word about Aurangzeb's Farman to build the Temple and allocation of the villages and funds for its maintenance.

The most shocking thing was the act of Information Officer who published a booklet about the Temples of Chitrakoot but no mention of Aurangzeb's farman.

Thereafter, I wrote many letters to the information office in Lucknow but never any reply was received. I mentioned this to the then Collector of Allahabad but he also did not say anything. Thereafter, I wrote an article on Swami Tulsidas in which I mentioned the Chitrakoots Balaji Temple having been built on the orders of Aurangzeb. The Article was published in 'Bharat', Hindi Daily but the portion of Aurangzeb's details were deleted from being published. Even the information of help and grant of many villages by Aurangzeb to Banaras Temples was not published."

All positive and true information about Muslims are suppressed and all negative information about Muslims even if they are false are prominently highlighted by the media be it print media or audio and visual media of the country. It is a deep routed conspiracy to create and maintain the Wedge between Hindus and Muslims. The fact that Muslims faught the Britishers and Hindus were supporters of Britishers in India is covered under the thick layers of Archives and the public is kept in dark.

My efforts has shown altogether a different picture and has convinced me, which I convey here with pride, and confidence, to the Muslims of India specially, and of the world in General and to the future generation of Muslims that your fore-fathers had nursed the honour of the un-divided Watan-e-Azeem Hindustan with their pure blood and sincerity of Nationalism with no vested interest of power or gain. You should be proud of your past and forge ahead with greater conviction of Nationalism in future and do not be cowed down by wrong and malicious propaganda against your Millat by narrow minded people.

By this humble effort I have tried to dig out a small portion, out of the huge buried ("Dafan"). History about the role of Muslims in the Movement of Independence for India. I have concentrated here, only on one region i.e. Patna Division as it existed in 1857 and the role of village Mohammedpur, District Azamgarh and its great son Maulana Peer Ali Khan. What happened in other parts of India other than Patna Division and Azamgarh is given in brief and hope some one will take up the cause of such Martyrs and bring them to limelight for the future generation to know their past.

The Islamic research institutions such as, "Majlise Tehqeequat-wa-Nashriat-e-Islam" in Nadwatul Uloon Lucknow has undertaken the job of digging out the role of Muslim Ulema in the Independence movement of India. But the role of common men out of Muslim community also needs special research and enlightenment for the world to know the truth. Here I have tried to "Excavate", I named this book "Excavation of Truth" and not "Discovery of Truth" because what I have written is already existed and nothing new has been discovered. I have just dug out the buried facts which all-along were being kept away from the people of this country and the new and future generations.

2

Peer Ali Khan, His Background and How He Came in Contact of Mir Abdullah the Richest Banker of Azeemabad/Patna

Peer Ali Khan the Mujahid-e-Azadi, the crusader against the British tyrannical rule in India, was born in the village "Mohammedpur" in the District of Azamgarh, U.P. India in 1820 AD. He sacrificed his life for the un-grateful and thankless people of the Country-India, and remained an unsung Hero of the Country.

Patna Division prior to 1857 as was defined by the Government of East India Company, Comprised of Patna, Gaya, Shahabad, Champaran, Saran and Trihut, through which River Ganga was flowing, bifurcated it from West to East. The Bihar State up to the South of Gorakhpur in U.P. touching the Eastern/ Northern bank of River Ghaghra was in Bengal Province. Earlier it was being ruled by Nawab Sirajuddaula till 23rd June, 1757. West and South of River Ghaghra was Eastern/ Northern border of Oudh.

William Taylor was the Commissioner of Patna Division since 1853 and continued till he was removed after 1857 rebellion had its Headquarter at Patna. Maula Baksh was the Deputy Commissioner of Patna, J.M. Lewis was the D.M. and Captain Rettrey was the S.P. of Patna. James Frederick Halliday was the Lt. Governor of Bengal Province and Sir George Canning Frederick was the Governor-General of East India Company.

Peer Ali's father Mehar Ali Khan was a poor peasant having migrated to Mohammedpur from another village—"Khadwari" about 10 kms west of Mohammedpur and settled and joined his maternal grandfather (*Nana*) who did not have any male issue.

Mehar Ali Khan had two sons, Nasrullah Khan elder and Peer Ali Khan younger.

The agricultural landholding which Mehar Ali had inherited from his maternal grandfather was very small and out of its produce their family could hardly manage to meet both ends.

The elders of village Mohammedpur have been narrating with pride that right from his childhood Peer Ali Khan had the passion to gain knowledge and education and was a very brave lad. The financial position of his father was not such by which he could have been sent to a School for education.

Peer Ali Khan at the age of about 7/8 years i.e. in 1827 or in 1828 AD, left his house. He kept on moving towards East of the District Azamgarh and some how reached at the out skirt of Patna City. It was summer season and to escape the scorching heat, and to rest, he slept under a *Banyan Tree*. He was suddenly woken up when he heard some voices. He saw that a *Qafila* with some armed sepoys and a "Palki" (a medieval carriage with box like cabin having log on two side carried by two to three persons in which Zameendars/Jagirdars or other rich persons used to travel) was heading towards the same Banyan Tree. Being scared of the Sepoys and other people accompanying the *Palki* he found no other escape and climbed on the Banyan Tree.

The *Qafila* after reaching under the tree stopped. People following the *Qafila* got busy in service of the person traveling in the *Palki*. He was Nawab Mir Abdullah a very rich Banker of Azeemabad (Patna). He had the wealth accumulated for over three generations of his ancestors beside having made huge money out of money-lending and purchase of Jageers and Zameendari in and around Azeemabad. Most of the old Zameendars were in heavy debts and their Zameendarees were being confiscated by the East India Company due to non-payment of Government dues. He found a very handy source of income and started the business of money-lending and financing to these Zameendars as well as Britishers. (Britishers called him Banker). In this business Mir Abdullah minted money and became still richer and also developed close relations with the high-ups in the East India

Company in Bengal and Bihar, specially with James Fredrick Halliday the then Lt. Governor of Bengal Province and Sir George Canning the Governor-General.

While Peer Ali Khan was sitting on the Banyan Tree un-noticed by the *Qafila.* He was observing the activities of the people on the ground.

Peer Ali Khan, saw that few of them were very nervous, because while trying to clean the *pipe* of the *Hukqa* with a shrub stick (*Sarkanda*), it broke and stuck in the pipe. They were not able to remove it from the *Hukqa pipe* and the Nawab Saheb wanted the *Hukqa* desperately.

Peer Ali Khan mustered courage and spoke from the place he was sitting on the tree, "if you people do not beat me I will remove it." (*Agar aap log mujhko maren nahin to main isko nikal doon*). All the people including Nawab Mir Abdullah were surprised to hear the voice from the top of the tree as no one saw him on the tree. The Nawab asked Peer Ali Khan to come down and assured him that no one will harm him. Peer Ali Khan got down from the tree and asked for a knife and cut the edge of the *Hukqa* pipe by about ¼" of the inch and pulled the cleaner, stick by his teeth. Seeing the intelligence of the child the Nawab Mir Abdullah was impressed and asked Peer Ali Khan, as to how and why he was in such a secluded place all alone. After knowing the interest of Peer Ali Khan and his intelligence he took Peer Ali Khan along with him. The Nawab Mir Abdullah groomed Peer Ali Khan as an educated person in Urdu, Persian and Arabic and a self-respecting young man with passion to fight against the Britishers and to throw them out form the Indian soil so that they may not enslave the country. This shows the dual personality of Mir Abdullah as apparently he was friend of British, but inwardly he was keen to some how throw the Britishers out of the country. But at the same time he did not want to put his family in danger.

Peer Ali Khan and the youngest son of Mir Abdullah, Saiyed Lootf Ali were brought up under direct supervision of Mir Abdullah. They later proved themselves as strong anti-British and pro-nationalist. This proves that Mir Abdullah was also of the same opinion and groomed Peer Ali Khan as a Mujahid against British rule.

3

The Background of Mir Abdullah and His Sons and Peer Ali's Grooming in His House

In the book "Karwan-e-Raft" published by Khudabaksh Oriental Public Library Patna in 1995, the writer Naqi Ahmed Irshad wrote that he contacted two of the known family members of Mir Abdullah, Saiyed Waris Ismail and Saiyed Ghazanfar Nawab both resident of Karachi and requested them to send the details of their family members. Both of them sent the detailed description of their family. Saiyed Waris Ismail died on 5th December, 1986 and Saiyed Ghazanfar Nawab in November 1987 both in Karachi. Thereafter, another member of the family Saiyed Masoom Raza Kazmi supplied the Family tree and details of properties in Pargana Balkhura from the National Archives.

According to the said book Saiyed Mir Abdullah's family begins from Saiyed Hasan Rizvi who was said to be a General in the Army of Nadir Shah. Saiyed Hasan Rizvi, had a son Saiyed Razi who also had a son Saiyed Murtuza.

Mir Abdulla was the son of Saiyed Murtuza i.e. great grand son of Saiyed Hasan Rizvi.

Naqi Ahmed Irshad in "Karwan-e Rafta" has given details of the future generations of Mir Abdulla. He had four sons. Nawab Mir Abdullah was resident of Katra Manakpur, Allahabad (in 1793 AD-1200 H). He used to be in attendance (in the Book it is written "Haziree Dete The") before one Hadi Ali Khan E.I.L. of East India Company in Katra Manakpur which was the Commissionery of Moghal period and was the Criminal Court of British Government. Hadi Ali Khan had three sons and five unmarried daughters.

It appears that Saiyed Hadi Ali married one of his five daughters to Mir Abdullah and advised him to settle in Azeemabad (Waride Azeemabad Hue) in 1801 AD in a Haweli known as "Gurji Mohsin Khan" where Mir Abdullah stayed till 1805 A.D. Mir Abdullah built another Haweli called "Bari Haweli" and shifted there in 1805 A.D. Mir Abdullah was already a very rich person from the wealth which he had inherited from his last three generation right from Saiyed Hasan Rizvi the General of Nadir Shah's Army. In short Mir Abdullah was a born rich man and lived like Nawab in Azeemabad (Patna) by acquiring large number of Zameendari, but he was not a designated Nawab or Jagirdar.

The book "Karvan-e-Rafta" shows that the family of Mir Abdullah was "Saiyed", but p. 189 of the said book the Shajra-e-Nasab of Mir Abdullah, with the name of his son Saiyed Lootf Ali the title (Khan) has been attached. Similarly, p. 190 with the name of Saiyed Mehdi Ali the title (Khan) has been attached followed by at other pages with the names of almost each subsequent person's name of his family "Khan" has been attached. It appears the family adopted the title of "Khan" which is very rarely done specially by Saiyeds, why? is not clear from the said book. Saiyed Mehdi Ali Khan had two sons and a daughter. The second son was Nawab Bahadur Saiyed Welayat Ali Khan who was virtually the agent of Britishers. Rest of the family members from the three sons of Mir Abdullah except Saiyed Lootf Ali Khan were neither anti-Britishers nor too close to them. However, Saiyed Lootf Ali Khan the youngest son of Mir Abdullah who was born in 1820 A.D. and was of the same age of Peer Ali Khan who also happened to have born in 1820 were staunch anti Britishers.

It was only Saiyed Lootf Ali Khan who stayed with Mir Abdullah in Bari Haweli and other three sons were staying independently separate from their father Mir Abdullah. Peer Ali Khan stayed in Mir Abdulla's Haweli till he completed his education and thereafter he stayed independently apparently with no connection with Mir Abdullah and his family.

In those days East India Company was badly in need of funds to meet the expenses of Wars, in Burma, China, Malaya and Singapore. To generate the funds they started Mahalwari as well as *ISTEMRARI Bandobast* (settlement) of the Agricultural land. The confiscated Zameendarees from old Zameendars who had defaulted in payment of Revenue Taxes and then re-sell or auction them to generate funds.

Mir Abdullah found it a golden opportunity to acquire those confiscated Zameendars. He also obtained some Zameendaris in the benami name of his Karinda "Gokul Chand". In this connection reference is made to a letter of the collector Patna being No. 773 dated 14.06.1822 which the Collector wrote to the President Revenue Board–Calcutta.

(Ref. "Karwan-e-Rafta")

Mir Abdullah had acquired property/Zameendari/Jageers worth crores of rupees on the strength of his wealth and also by force of Arms because he had almost purchased the high up in East India Company by heavily bribing them. Mir Abdullah died in 1265 (H) (1859 A.D.) in Patna and was buried in his self acquired property/ Burial ground in Tulsi Mandi (Aggam Kuwan).

(Ref. "Karwan-e-Rafta")

Nawab Mir Abdullah had four sons. Eldest was Mehdi Ali (1207 H to 1266 H/ 1800 A.D. to 1860 A.D.), then Saiyed Mohammed Ali (1212 H to 1238 H/ 1805 AD to 1831 AD), Saiyed Qasim Ali (1222 H to 1287 H/ 1815 AD to 1881 AD) and Saiyed Lootf Ali Khan (1227 H to 1307 H/ 1820 AD to 1901 AD).

Saiyed Welayat Ali Khan s/o Saiyed Mehdi Ali eldest son of Mir Abdullah and grand sons of Mir Abdullah was very loyal to East India Company. He was the second son of Saiyed Mehdi Ali Khan and nephew of Saiyed Lootf Ali Khan, still when, William Taylor arrested Lootf Ali Khan in the night of 5th July, 1857 and was after his blood, Welayat Ali Khan did not do anything to help Lootf Ali Khan rather was by the side of Britishers for which he was bestowed the honour of "Nawab Bahadur" and later as "Order of the Indian Empire". On the other hand, Peer Ali Khan who was very close associate of Lootf Ali Khan inspite of extreme torture from Taylor did not utter a word by which Lootf Ali could have been put to gallows. Lootf Ali Khan was arrested because Shekh Ghaseeta who was arrested alongwith Peer Ali Khan was the employee of Lootf Ali Khan and his mother was the Aya of Lootf Ali's mother.

Late Shri Maqbool Ahmad Khan the maternal cousin of my father from the knowledge obtained from Maulvi Mohd. Naeem Khan, my great grandfather narrated to me that Peer Ali Khan was a very intelligent and witty person. He used to narrate to me many incidence about Peer Ali Khan. In one of the incidence which took place while Peer Ali was living with Mir Abdullah, completely changed, the very appearance of Peer Ali Khan. The incidence is narrated as under:

> "While Peer Ali Khan was staying with the Nawab oneday he was writhing with severe stomach pain. The Nawab Mir Abdullah directed Peer Ali Khan to go to a particular room of the 'Bari Haweli' and take two tablets (*Goli*) from an earthen pot and eat it. While Peer Ali Khan was gone to take the medicine the Nawab Mir Abdullah remembered that adjacent to the pot there was another pot in which poisonous tablets were kept. The Nawab rushed to the spot but it was too late as Peer Ali Khan had already swallowed two tablets out of the poisonous one instead the one suggested by the Nawab. The Nawab immediately made Peer Ali Khan to drink lot of *Pure Ghee*. Thus, the effect of the poison was diluted. However, its after effects made Peer Ali Khan's eyes permanently red and there was a permanent glow on his face and made him look robust. This further enhanced the personality of Peer Ali Khan like a direct descendant of Afghan Pathan. Though he belonged to Afghan race as the villages, like Khadwari, Mohammedpur are from Afghan migratory."

The above narrative by late Maqbool Ahmad Khan gets support from the following observations of Thomas Rettray about Peer Ali Khan:

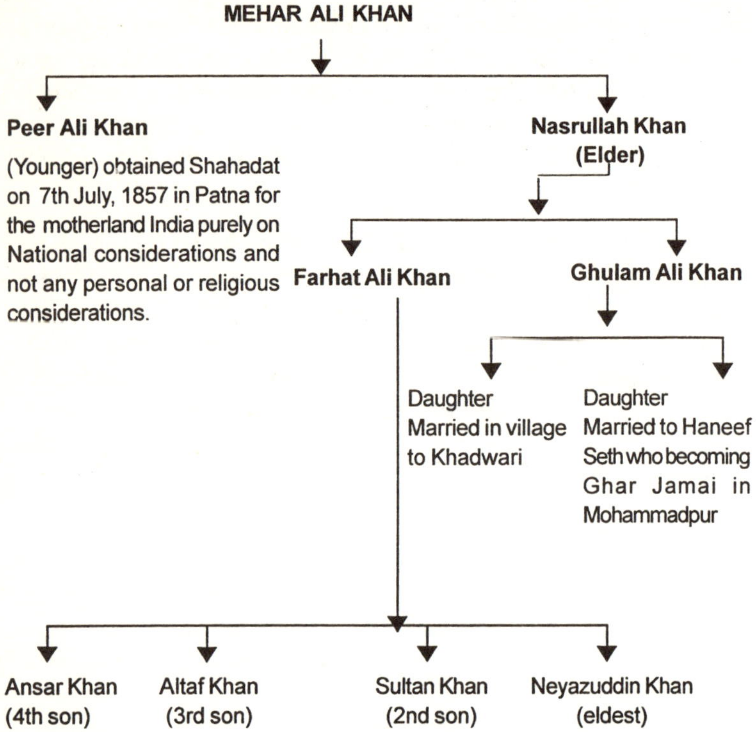

> "He was a strong, muscular, bull necked with expression of countenance."

Peer Ali Khan was not married and remained bachelor till his hanging at the prime of his life at the age of 37 years. However, Nasrullah Khan the elder brother of Peer Ali Khan was married and had a son, Maulvi Habeeb Khan who further had two sons—Ghulam Ali Khan (elder) and Farhat Ali Khan (younger). Ghulam Ali Khan had only two daughters—elder one was married to one Mohd. Haneef who settled in the village Mohammedpur as *Ghar Jamai* and later established Supari Business in Nall Bazaar/ Bhindi Bazar, Mumbai and was popularly known as Haneef Seth. Haneef Seth had two sons—Shabbeer and Ayub and 4 daughters. The other younger daughter of Ghulam Ali Khan was married in Khadwari in the same family branch to which the father of Peer Ali belonged.

Farhat Ali Khan the younger brother of Ghulam Ali (the nephew of Peer Ali Khan) has four sons and are living in Mohammedpur but are poor and financially not very sound. The family tree of Peer Ali Khan is as data:

Peer Ali Khan while in Patna used to visit his family in Mohammedpur however, avoided giving any detail of his village and its people including his family to anyone in Patna, with the intention to save them from the British backlash. He was engaged in "JEHAD" against Britishers. Late Shri Maqbool Ahmad Khan on the basis of his knowledge from my great grandfather Maulvi Mohd. Naeem Khan who was a young man in 1857 and was also very much involved in the movement against Britishers told me that the village Mohammedpur and its people were saved because on the advice of the Subedar Baba people of Mohammedpur disowned any link with Peer Ali Khan with the village and based on this information to the authorities the village and its people were saved.

Willam Taylor in his book "Our Crisis" in Chapter IX mentions, about Peer Ali:

"After this defiance, he joined his manacled hands, and said, with the utmost politeness, as if he was on the best of terms with himself, the world, and me,'I have something to ask'—'Well, what is it?' Speak, 'My house'—'It will be razed to the ground,'—'My property?'—'It will be confiscated'—'My children,' and here for the first time, his voice faltered and his tone betrayed emotion—On my asking him where his children were, he said they were in Oude."

From the said statement of Peer Ali "Oudh" and the letters confiscated from his shop having regular correspondence with Maseehuzzaman of Lucknow, Taylor assumed that he was from Lucknow, without realizing that, Peer Ali said, "Oudh" and not Lucknow. Oudh was a province and a separate territory from that of Bengal and Behar and had large number of other districts which included Azamgarh also.

4

Peer Ali Khan and His Association with Saiyed Lootf Ali Khan the Youngest Son of Mir Abdullah and Other Associates and their Involvement in the 1857 Revolt in Patna Division and the Activities of William Taylor, the Commissioner of Patna Division His Repressive Actions and His Removal as Commissioner. The Atrocities by Britishers

After Peer Ali Khan grew up he was helped by Mir Abdullah and Lootf Ali Khan to acquire a shop on the main Road of Patna near the Haweli of Padri. This was part of the scheme between Mir Abdullah, Saiyed Lootf Ali and Peer Ali Khan so that the activities of Peer Ali Khan remain secret apparently with no connection with Mir Abdullah and Lootf Ali Khan, Peer Ali Khan spear headed his campaign against the Britishers from the said shop apparently independently with no connection with Mir Abdullah or Saiyed Lootf Ali Khan. Peer Ali Khan attained the martyrdom on 7th July, 1857. Mir Abdullah's relations with the Lt. Governor of Bengal James Frederick Halliday and Sir George Canning the Governor-General plus the wealth saved his son Lootf Ali Khan from the gallows inspite of all the efforts of William Taylor. Mir Abdullah could not survive long thereafter and died in 1859.

Peer Ali Khan as a cover job used to sell hand written books and was known as the book-seller. His shop was situated next to the Haweli of "Padri" at the main Highway leading to the East, from Bankipura to Bakhtiarpur. The Padri was the main priest of the Cathedral, built with the permission of the Moghal King Jehangir and the "Bell' installed thereon was gifted by a subsequent Moghal King, probably Shahjahan.

Peer Ali Khan in association with his friends had been generating revolt against the British much before the revolt broke out in Shahabad, Gaya and Danapur Cantonment or even the Sepoy movements from Bairakhpor and Meerut etc. Peer Ali Khan set a very high moral tone and stiff standard for martyrs in modern India which fact has been recognized by the Britishers themselves including William Taylor who was responsible to hang Peer Ali Khan. He was arrested on 4th July, 1857 tortured for four days and then charged with the killing of Dr. Lloyel (the assistant to the Agent of the opium Godown in Patna), waging war against the Crown and was hanged in Patna on 7th July, 1857 by William Taylor.

Events of the revolt in 1857 in Patna Division is recorded in various books and documents. One of the books is titled "Patna Crisis" by W. Taylor the Commissioner of Patna Division and published by James Nisbet and Company, London, 1858. Later in 1882 the revised Editions of the same book was published by W.H. Allen and Co., London with the title of "Patna Crisis—Three Months at Patna."

In his book, "Thirty-eight Years in India" in Vol. II, p. 238, Taylor writes:

> "I will first, however, mention that short narrative of the events which transpired during three-first months of the Mutiny, was published by me shortly after the occurrence, in a little book, of which the first edition was called 'Our Crisis' and the second (re-published by M/s. Nisbet and Co. on the recommendation of Dr. Duff), with the title of 'The Patna Crisis'. This little broucher, being written while I was still in the service, was necessarily circumspect and moderate in its tone and passed over many minor incidents which, though important in themselves, it would have

> been unsafe and perhaps unwise to lay before the public; it contains, however, an accurate though brief summary of the events as they occurred. Those who wish to have a correct idea of our position, from the commencement of our troubles to the day of my suspension from office. It will be too long to insert here, but which for the third time has been reprinted, by W.H. Allen and Co. London."

The publishers, Nisbet and Co. as well as W.H. Allen and Co., both are no more into existence and their where about is not known. Even the book "Our Crisis", "Patna Crises" and "Patna Crisis—Three Months at Patna" are not available in Indian Archives and prominent libraries. It might be lying buried in some unknown libraries.

I tried with "School of Oriental and African Studies, Brunei Gallery Building, 10 Thornhangh Street, London, WCIH-OXG" but one Mr. Joe Burridge SOAS/ Probstathains, gave the reply as under:

> "Dear Mr. Khan, we have about 800 antiquarian Indian Books in stock at the moment, many of which cover the period you are researching. You can browse and buy them from this address."

He did not confirm whether the book "Patna Crisis—Three Months at Patna" by William Taylor was available or not . His mail address is as under: "From Joe Burridge" — <jbbo@soas.ac.uk>

The availability of the book, "Patna Crisis" was provided to me by Mr. Mario Kropf through my son Khan Ahmad Adeel. The text of message of Mr. Mario dated 28.12.2006 is as under:

> Dear Adeel,
>
> Subject: *Re Contents of Book Patna Crisis*
>
> The text you refer came from a book "The Patna Crisis: or Three Months at Patna during the insurgency of 1857/ by William Taylor"
>
> A copy is in the library of Princeton University,

Princeton University Library,

One Washington Road, Princeton,

New Jersey 08544,
U.S.A. Phone : 609-258-1470 Fax: 609-258-0441

The printout details were obtained by browsing from the books of A.K. Biswas. A typed copy of the book "Our Crisis—Three Months at Patna" is available at Khunda Baksh Library, Patna.

In the said books William Taylor who was responsible to give Peer Ali Khan the death sentence, has described the bravery and calm and composed attitude of Peer Ali Khan even on the gallows (Takhta-e-daar). He himself described Peer Ali Khan in his book and letters written to his superiors. Just before he was to be hanged on 7th July, 1857. Taylor asked Peer Ali Khan:

> "If you (Peer Ali) disclose the names of all other persons who are/ were associated with you and all about your family and their where about I will spare your life."

Taylor quoted Peer Ali Khan's words in reply to his offer:

> "There are some occasions, on which it is good to give up life and get sacrificed, thousands others will fill the place."

The Indian historians, specially Muslim historians did not find, Peer Ali Khan worth mention any where even as a freedom fighter when he was the leader of the independence movement in Patna Division as recognized by the British administration. Saiyed Welayat Ali Khan who was a recognized informer of William Taylor, the then Commissioner of Patna Division, and for his services to Britishers and Ghaddari to the Nation, the Britishers, decorated him with the title of, "Order of Indian Empire", and a Muslim writer Shad Azeemabadi found it necessary to publish his "Swaneh Umri" life History and for Peer Ali Khan Shaheed-e-Watan a small novel published by "Maktaba Jamia", New Delhi.

A.K. Biswas in his book "Unsung Martyrs of 1857" and in its abridged edition by I.K. Shukla while paying homage to the Martyrs such as Peer Ali Khan recorded:

"The sacrifices of a dedicated band of patriots led by Peer Ali Khan of Patna and of the lowly Rajwar community of Rajgir during the revolt of Hindustan in 1857-58 remain neglected in the histography of our First war of Independence against the Brits. This homage sets the record straight about our real martyrs and heroes."

Inspite of extreme torture and lurement to his life, Peer Ali Khan did not disclose the names of any of his supporters nor his antecedents. Taylor could not get even a word from Peer Ali Khan about his connection with Lootf Ali Khan and Mir Abdullah. Lootf Ali Khan and Peer Ali Khan both of the same age and were groomed alike by Mir Abdullah were very loyal to each other. Peer Ali Khan a brave and grateful, in the true tradition of a Pathan, even at the cost of his life, did not disclose the name of his mentor nor disclosed the place of his origin, the village he belonged or his family. Peer Ali's other strong and close associates in his Jehaad against Britishers were Maulvi Ali Kareem a rich Zameendar of Dausi, and Waris Ali a Sepoy in the Rank of Jamadar of British Army, at Trihoot and Maseehuzzaman of Lucknow an associate of Maulvi Ahmadullah Madrasi.

When Taylor could not find out anything from Peer Ali Khan inspite of interrogation and torture for 4 days i.e. 4th, 5th, 6th and 7th July, 1857, after his arrest on 4th July, 1857, he got him hanged on 7th July, 1857. His 16 other followers were already hanged on 5th July, 1857 itself, 17 were imprisoned with hard labour and two transported to penal settlements. No details is available as to how many were killed by the Sikh and British soldiers who were deployed by William Taylor under the command of Rettray who ransacked the entire city of Patna for days together. After Peer Ali's hanging Taylor ordered that all those connected with Peer Ali be killed and their properties destroyed. In the words of Taylor:

"I (Taylor) have ordered his (Peer Ali's) along with all those connected with him (Peer Ali) killed and, their houses to be razed to the ground and a post be placed on the spot with a notice, stating that he (Peer Ali) and sixteen others of his (Peer Ali's) accomplices have been hanged ...., if such a combination and conspiracy is again discovered, I (Taylor) will make all the Ward responsible."

(Page 408, "A History of Indian Mutiny", 3rd Vol. by G. W. Forrest) from "Patna Crisis—Three Months at Patna" by William Taylor.

p. 407, Vol-III, G.W. Forrest noted:

"On the information of one of the wounded, Peer Ali Khan, a Mohammedan bookseller, was arrested, 'after some resistance'. His house searched, and a considerable quantity of arms and treasonable correspondence found in it. He was tried, convicted, and hanged."

Taylor in his report recorded: as reproduced, p. 408 in the Book of G.W. Forrest, 3rd Volume; described the character of Waris Ali another Associate of Peer Ali Khan as under:

"On 23rd June, 1857, a native police officer was arrested at Trihoot, in the very act of conducting a treasonable correspondence with some disaffected Mohammedans of Patna, and sent there to be tried. I postponed his trial for two or three days after his arrival and had several private interviews with him, hoping by such means to elicit information; but he was evidently not in the secrets of the leaders, as he could tell me nothing more than what I already knew from other sources; and he was in such excessive alarm and despair, that I am convinced he would have done anything to save his life. When speaking in private with me, he implored me to tell him whether there was any way in which his life could be spared. I said 'yes' and his eyes opened with unmistakable delight; ....I told him, 'I will make a bargain with you; give me three lives, and I will give you your's. He then told me all the names I already knew, but could disclose nothing further. He was evidently not clever enough to be a confident."

I think Waris Ali was making fool of Taylor throughout. Because he was arrested on 23rd June, 1857 and Peer Ali Khan was arrested only on 4th July, 1857 that too after having organized and lead the revolt on 3rd July, 1857 shows that Waris Ali did not give any information about Peer Ali Khan prior to Peer Ali's arrest.

The above shows the brave character of Peer Ali Khan and his supporters, who at the offer of Taylor to save their lives preferred the gallows rather betraying their friends' and followers' confidence.

Taylor directed Maula Baksh the Deputy Commissioner of Patna to find out each and every detail of Peer Ali Khan. However, Maula Baksh could not provide much details about Peer Ali Khan except that he was a poor book-seller and had come to Patna from Lucknow, but not much details could be found. Even the link of Peer Ali Khan with Nawab Mir Abdullah and Nawab Lootf Ali Khan in whose house he was brought up as a young man from the age of 7/8 years in Azeemabad, Patna itself, could not be found.

In fact late Maqbool Ahmad Khan told me that an enquiry was received at the Thana, Gambhirpur about Peer Ali Khan's connection with the village. He also told me that one person of the village Mohammedpur who was working on the rank of Subedar in British army/ Police played a decisive role to save the village Mohammedpur and the family of Peer Ali Khan. Subedar was the highest rank to which any native person could be promoted or appointed during East India Co.'s rule and the initial period of British rule. He used his influence being in British Army and on the highest post to which any native could reach plus the bribe to the concerned British enquiry Officer. Thereafter, a report was sent to Patna that Peer Ali Khan had no connection with the village Mohammedpur. Thus, the Subedar Baba played a very important role and saved the village Mohammedpur and its people from total destruction and mass murder in the hands of Britishers. Subedar Baba had a son named Maula Baksh. Maula Baksh also had a son named Maulvi Mustafa who had only a daughter. Subedar Baba was allotted *fief* (agricultural land free of land revenue) in the village "Nagaraiya – Jahanpur" south of the village Mohammedpur across Manghai River. The said property was somehow captured by Mr. Amjad Ali Khan Vakil and Mr. Ghulam Rabbani of the village Mohammedpur by depriving the only daughter of Maulvi Mustafa Khan, how, nobody knows? In my childhood I used to see late Asad Ali Khan father of Mr. Amjad and Ghulam Rabbani carrying food for Maulvi Mustafa Khan. Here it will not be out of place to mention that late Asad Ali Khan was working in Indian Railways as track inspector and was dismissed because he once helped Pandit Nehru to escape the arrest by the Police, and transported him and his companion on his track trolly. Pandit Nehru in return provided all expenses for the education of Amjad Ali Khan who acquired the Law degree from B.H.U.

Given the option Taylor would have implemented his threat, not only to raze and burn the entire village Mohammedpur and the people would have been killed, but because he himself was removed from the post of Deputy Commissioner of Patna alongwith Mr. Maula Baksh the village Mohammedpur escaped the total disaster by British.

At page 398 of the book of G.W. Forrest, 4th Vol. He has described the savagery nature of William Taylor:

> "Mr. William Taylor, a man of considerable cultured. He was, however, prone to associate the elevation of his own personality with his administrative measures. He was quick and clever, but his judgement was not always clear, and he had not a sufficient regard for system. Taylor was to overawe the fanatics and suspected classes by repressive measures, which, however, endangered as much hatred as fear."

The arrogant and autocratic style of working of Taylor can be judged from the reply he gave to Lord Canning on his simple advice:

> "The part of a wise government, is to keep such population......... in a Loyal frame of mind."
>
> Taylor replied:
>
> "As long as I have breath in my body, I will pursue no other policy than that which I have been following—not only for the reason of expediency and policy above stated, but because it is just. Justice, and that as stern and inflexible

as Law and might can make it, I will deal out. But I will never allow an angry or indiscriminating act or word to proceed from the Government of India as long as I am responsible for it."

Thus, Taylor with his autocratic style of working and helped by Maula Baksh brought a situation where his critics which included the Lt. Governor found the excuse to sack him.

Charles Allen in his book "God's Terrorist", pp. 153-154 writes:

"On 5th August, 1857, he (Frederick Halliday the Lft. Governor) informed the Governor-General that, it appears from a letter just received from Mr. Taylor, that whilst apparently under the influence of a panic, he has ordered officials at all the stations in his division to abandon their posts and fall back in Danapore..........."

"On the basis of Halliday's report, which cited Taylor's withdrawl orders......... Lord Canning confirmed William Taylor's removal on three grounds, i.e. showing great want of calmness and firmness; issuing an order quite beyond his competency; and interfering with the military authorities."

"Mr. Justice Farquharson, one of the most persistent critics of Taylor was appointed acting Commissioner, pending the arrival of Taylor's replacement, Mr. Edward Samuells."

"Samuells arrived bringing with him his own deputy to replace William Taylor's, deputy and right hand man, Dewan Maula Baksh, who was also dismissed on the grounds that he and a Muslims banker (Saiyed Welayat Ali Khan) who had rendered great assistance in the arrest of the Wahabee leaders by William Taylor, and that it was motivated by jealously."

"One of the 1st action of the new commissioner was to release the three Wahabee leaders, accompanied by the profuse apologies of the Government of India with a proclamation that they were innocent and inoffensive men."

> "The Commissioner then held a conciliatory, let bygones, be bygones, picnic to honour the Wahabees."

Besides the above, further savagery acts of Britishers against Indians has been recorded by Karl Marx in his letter dated 04.09.1857, published in the *New York Daily Tribune* in Issue No. 5119 of September 16, 1857 as recorded in the book titled, "The First Indian War of Independence 1857-59" by K. Marx and F. Engels published by Foreign Languages publishing House, Moscow based on the Russian edition prepared by the Institute of Marxism–Leninism of the C.C., C.P.S.U. in 1959.

The extract of the said letter of K. Marx dated 04.09.1857, pp. 92-93 of the said book is as under:

> "The letters of the British officers are redolent (smelling strongly) of malignity (cruelty). An officer writing from Peshawar gives a description of the disarming of the 10th irregular cavalry for not charging the 55th Native infantry, when ordered to do so. He exults in the fact that they were not only disarmed, but stripped of their coats and boots, and after having received 12d. per man, were marched down to the river side, and there embarked in boats and sent down the Indus; where the water is delighted to expect every mother's son will have a chance of being drowned in the rapids. Another writer informs us that some inhabitants of Peshawar having caused a night alarm by exploding little mines of gunpowder in honour of a wedding (a national custom), the persons concerned were tied up next morning and *received such a flogging as they will not easily forget.*
>
> "News received from Pindee that three native chiefs were plotting. Sir John Lawrance replied by message ordering a sepoy to attend to the meeting. On the sepoy's report, Sir John sent a second message, 'Hang them'. The Chiefs were hanged."
>
> "An officer in the civil service from Allahabad, writes: 'We have power of life and death in our hands, and we assure you we spare none'."

"Another from the same place: 'Not a day passes but we string up from ten to fifteen of them (non-combatants)'."

"One exulted officer writes: 'Holmes is hanging them by the score, like a brick.' Another in allusion to the summary hanging of a large body of the natives: 'Then our fun commenced.' A third 'we hold court-martials on horseback, and every nigger (black person) we meet with we either string up or shoot' From Bananas we were informed that thirty Zamindars were hanged on the mere suspicion of sympathizing with their own country men, and whole villages were burned down on the same plea. An officer from Bananas, whose letter is printed in the London Times says: 'The European troops have become fiends (very cruel).when opposed to Natives'."

"And then it should not be forgotten that, while the cruelties of the English are related as acts of martial vigour, told simply, rapidly, without dwelling on disgusting details, the outrages of the natives, shocking as they are, are still deliberately exaggerated."

Karl Marx refuted in his article published in *New York Tribune* dated 15.04.1858, the allegations of Britishers that native soldiers dishonoured many English women:

"After the rebellion was suppressed, despite the English arduously trying to find evidence against the rebels for molesting English women nothing by way of evidence could be found. Yet the cry that native homes dishonoured our women, was a very important piece of hate propaganda spread in English against the Mutineers and used to justify all barbarities perpetrated."

Dr. B.M. Sankhdher in an article from the "Archives" wrote interalia in National Herald Daily dt. 21.10.2006 with the title of "British Vulgarity":

"British Officials indulged in worst kind of vulgarity, indecency and lack of civilized behaviour."

> "Some of the Co.'s officials, mad with power, behaved, savage and beastly manner."

The above description in the words of Britishers themselves, are proof enough, that if Peer Ali Khan would have given the names of his associates, supporters, and his antecedents, no amount of relations of Mir Abdullah with British high ups, or his bribes to them would have saved Saiyed Lootf Ali Khan, and the village Mohammedpur and its people, from the savagery acts of Britishers through William Taylor.

Here again I will quote Gautam Jetly out of his article:

> "As a nation of shop-keepers, England was famous for its bland food. The East was spicy. Seeing the native sensual lap of luxury, they followed suit. Not satisfied with money, and women, they now wanted land: Then their was greed. They were cruel and sadistic: the English race."

Similarly Fradric Engles also recalled that in 1870 the British in India violated all laws of war in killing the prisoners of war; and they did so by even imaginable, fiendish means, like hanging after biding their victims in contorted forms or – a special favourite-blowing the captives from mouths of their guns. Col. James Neill from early June 1857 committed horrible bouts of atrocities on each village or town. Every success of the British was marked by general massacre and plunder of civil populations. William Russell of London Times was a witness to the British loot of Lucknow in March, 1857, also slaughter of civilians, including women and children, wrought by British at Jhansi and neighbouring towns. The repression, trial and execution, confiscation of Lands and properties continued even after the end of Rebellion. Not only individuals but the whole families, whose members were suspected of having been involved in the Mutiny were deprived of their lands. Such confiscated lands were given to British families and such "Natives" who claimed to have rendered service to British against their own compatriots. The number native sepoys were reduced from 2,00,000 to 1,21,000 and the number of European soldiers was increased from 38,000 to 76,000. The salary of European soldier was several times more than native sepoys hence the burden on the Indian Tax payers increased many fold.

T.R.E. Homes in his Book "A History of Indian Mutiny", p. 185 mentions:

> "Taylor would not have been able to procure the evidence which he required against these men, if he had not been helped by three loyal natives Saiyed Welayat Ali Khan, Maula Baksh the Deputy Magistrate, and Hidayat Ali, the Subedar of the Sikh Corps."

William Taylor himself wrote in his book titled, "Thirty-eight Years in India", Volume II, p. 281:

> "It is gratifying to me to be able at this time to record the assistance I received from several of the respectable native residents of Patna, more especially from the following: Maha Rajah Bhoop Singh, Welayat Ali Khan, Sekh Ruza Hussain, Altoof Hussain, Roy Hurreekishen, Baboo Chooneelal and several others who have tendered their services, and expressed their willingness to be of use."

Since the removal of William Taylor and Maula Baksh Mr. Samuells got busy in the policy of "let bygone is bygone" no serious enquiry was made to find out details about Peer Ali Khan's antecedents, most probably at the influence of Mir Abdullah who was very close to Lft. Governor and Samuells, as it would have exposed Saiyed Lootf Ali Khan. Detailed information about Peer Ali Khan would have exposed Saiyed Lootf Ali and Mir Abdullah about their connection with Peer Ali Khan.

Taylor's uncontrolled villings of Muslims and summary trials and hangings of Muslims in Patna, convinced Mir Abdullah that so long Taylor will remain at the helm of Patna division he will not let the matter go only on the hanging of Peer Ali Khan and some of his associates hence he used his influence and money power to ensure that Taylor is removed as Commissioner of Patna. Mir Abdullah being the rich man must have generously bribed the Lt. Governor and the judge to save his son. This was possible only if the enquiry against Peer Ali Khan and his other associate who were already hanged was not pursued any further. The employees of East India Company right from top man to the lower order were very found of taking bribe. Dr. Moti Chand in his Book—"Kashi Ka Itihas" between pp. 250-75 has described as to how East India Company's officers and ex-employees were always ready to accept the bribe. Lord Clive was even disgraced by the Parliament of Britain on this score. Be that as it may, the people of village Mohammedpur escaped the total destruction as Taylor had planed and ordered immediately after the hanging of Peer Ali Khan, that "All those connected with him (Peer Ali) killed and their houses to be razed to the ground." Taylor was removed as Commissioner of Patna Division.

Taylor did not take his removal lightly but made his efforts right upto the Directors of East India Company in London, but the Lt. Governor Halliday not only did not let Taylor succeed but got him posted just to disgrace him, on the duty to check the spread of Malaria in the remote villages of East Bengal near Dhaka. Taylor himself described these facts in his autobiography.

"Thirty-eight Years in India", Vol. II, pp. 252-53.

"The Lt. Governor, with certain supplementary attributes suggested by the gentleman (Mr. Samuels) whom he appointed to succeed me (made the following statement to the East India Company).

First: Sir F. Halliday officially declared that 'there was 'no danger at Patna.'

Secondly: By Danapore Sepoys 'Mutiny was inconceivable.'

Then to delineate my character described my actions as:

1st: The sole danger of Patna was caused by my 'violent and unwise proceedings.'

2nd: That I 'lent myself to a thirst for reckless bloodshed.'

3rd: That I 'sentenced and executed men who were not convicted of any crime.'

4th: That I kept under arrest innocent and inoffensive 'gentlemen against whom there was no cause of complaint.'

5th: That I made myself the tool of worthless and designing traitors.

6th: That I showed a great want of calmness and firmness.

7th: That I interfered with the military authorities.

8th: That I concealed as much as possible my acts and intentions.

9th: That I was guilty of a 'quibble'.

10th: That I wrote 'frequent orders to major Eyre not to advance to the relief of Arrah.

11th: That I was under a panic.

12th: That I issued a 'disgraceful' order.

13th: And finally, that I created universal scandal and discontent by my measures."

At page 302 of the book "Memoirs of William Taylor" the memorandum submitted by Mr. Taylor to the British Government is reproduced where in he mentions:

"After my sudden removal from office by the then Lieutenant Governor of Bengal, Mr. Frederick Halliday, my successor in the Commissionership, Mr. Samuells, with the concurrence and approval of the Lieutenant Governor (in the official Blue book) described these men as "innocent and inoffensive," mere book-men, against whom there was no cause of suspicion, "and in the same letter, suggested that I had been induced to arrest them because of their loyalty, through the machinations of the men whom I had consulted viz. Saiyed Welayat Ali Khan, a wealthy resident of Patna and Dewan Maula Baksh, a Deputy Magistrate, my official subordinate."

William Taylor wrote that:

"At the time of my removal Dewan Maula Baksh, and Saiyed Welayat Ali Khan were considered by Mr. Samuell as deceitful traitors who made me (Taylor) tool for treasonous purposes. Later these very people were

> honoured by her Majestary Queen Victoria with the Title 'Star of India' (Maula Baksh) and 'Order of the Indian Empire' (Saiyed Welayat Ali Khan) and Haji Ahmadullah was sentenced to be hanged. In appeal their death sentence was converted to life imprisonment not on mercy but to avoid them becoming 'Hero' in the eyes of their followers."
>
> *(P. 233, Memoirs of William Taylor)*

Here Taylor did not mention in his Memoirs the letter of the Secretary of Government of Bengal dated 27.06.1857, where in the Secretary conveyed to him the displeasure of Lt. Governor on the style of Taylor's working and specifically pointed to him:

(a) You keep the Government wholly in dark for days together.

(b) Lt. Governor directed to say that he will supercede you by a person who will keep the Government informed.

(c) The Lt. Governor caution you against unnecessary harshness and against all illegal proceeding.

(d) You seem to have been acting in a very unusual and questionable manner.

(e) The strong dissatisfaction of the Lt. Governor at this mode of proceeding, on your part has already been very distinctly expressed to you.

(f) While you darkly intimate that you are adopting measures of great responsibility and importance, I am directed to say, quite intolerable.

(Pp. 404-05 the book Vol.-III, G.W. Forrest)

In defence of Taylor, Sir John Kaye writes in his book "History of Sepoy War", Vol. III, pp. 163-64, quoted at the footnote p. 404 of the G.W. Forrest, book Vol. III:

> "Not only was it his (Taylor's) wont to do his work in his own way without consulting anyone to do it first, and to write to Government afterwards-but sometimes in the hurry and crush of overwhelming business, he did it

without reporting it at all.......... But bureaucracy was still join to arrest that there could be no duty on the part of a public functionary more urgent than that of reporting his proceeding to Government. It is not too much to say that if this duty had been generally recognized we should have lost India."

The last sentence shows that according to Sir John Kaye enslaving India was more important than the discipline of the executives of the East India Company.

It appears that Mir Abdullah used his influence and money to see that no detailed enquiry about Peer Ali Khan is held and Mr. Samuells also decided not to pursue it since Peer Ali Khan was already hanged and there was no one to follow his case after the removal of William Taylor, and Maula Baksh. The Lt. Governor's office, may have advised Mr. Samuells to save Lootf Ali Khan. This could be the reason that the records of 1857 mutiny in Patna do not shed light on the exact place from where Peer Ali Khan belonged. Some called him Maulvi of Lucknow, some called him Maulvi of Delhi, A.K. Biswas called him "daunted son of Patna". It was found, from the papers confiscated from his shop that he was in constant touch with Maulvi Massih-Huz-Zaman of Lucknow and was close friend of Waris Ali of Delhi who was a Sepoy in Trihut in British Army in the post of Jamadar.

Charles Allen's book "God's Terrorist", pp. 144-45, mentions:

"On 3rd July a large mob waving banners, banging drums and chanting 'Deen! Deen!' attacked the Roman Catholic Mission, in the heart of the native town."

"A wounded rioter was seized and taken to the hospital to be treated. There Subedar Hidayat Ali, Rettary's second in command, gained his confidence and he began to talk. This led to the arrest of thirty-one alleged conspirators, including a book seller named Peer Ali Khan, noted for his enthusiasm for his religion and hatred of the English? Taylor already had information suggesting that Peer Ali was the leading member of a cell taking its orders from the rebels in Lucknow and now a bundle of letters found in his possession confirmed this. They had come from a fellow book-seller in Lucknow and contained instructions as to how Peer Ali was to further the cause of the "Fatteh Ooper Nesara" or victory over the Nazarenes. Peer Ali had also been charged with the task of persuading the leaders of the Wahabees in Patna to join the revolt, but in this he failed, probably because the Lucknow correspondent had urged that the rebels should join forces with all religious groups in India, even if that meant working with Shias and Hindus."

Here Charles Allen is wrong in assuming that Taylor already had all the above details prior to the arrest of Peer Ali Khan. Taylor for the first time came to know the name of Peer Ali Khan from the letter confiscated from Waris Ali Khan when he asked Maula Baksh to find out as who is this Peer Ali. It was few days thereafter Peer Ali went to Maulvi Ahmadullah to deliver some books where Saiyed Welayat Ali was also present and was alarmed after hearing the name of Peer Ali Khan, when Maulvi Ahmadullah called Peer Ali Khan by his name. After Peer Ali Khan left, Welayat Ali enquired from Maulvi Ahamadullah who this Peer Ali Khan was. Maulvi Ahmadullah told him that he was book-seller having his shop near Padri's Haweli and belongs to Lucknow. Saiyed Welayat Ali immediately left and went straight to William Taylor where Maula Baksh was also present and told Taylor about Peer Ali as to who he was and that he has come to Patna from Lucknow. Taylor still did not give Peer Ali Khan much importance and asked Maula Baksh to find out full details about Peer Ali but 1st arrest Ali Kareem. Thus Peer Ali was not disturbed till 3rd of July, 1857.

After having hanged Peer Ali Khan and his associates, Taylor's main efforts and concentration was to hang Saiyed Lootf Ali Khan who was a rich man and his connection with many supporters of Peer Ali Khan was known. Two of them were infact working in Lootf Ali's house. Still due to his father's relations and the wealth together helped Lootf Ali to escape the gallows.

After the failure of the 1857, Revolt the British established themselves and ruled upto 1947. After the Independence Movement of 1857 British Government passed a draconian law under which they could arrest any Indian and keep him/ them in Jail for life, without trial. This way the British Government made mass arrest of majority of Muslims and either hanged them or deported them to Andaman Nikobar Island for permanent abode away from their family. That is why the majority of inhabitants at Andaman and Nikobar are Muslims. This law continued till 14th August, 1947 i.e., till the day British rule remained over India. The brother of Peer Ali Khan, Nasrullah Khan or nephew Maulvi Habeeb Khan were too poor and could not dare to claim their blood relations with Peer Ali. Ghulam Ali Khan died before 15th August, 1947. Farhat Ali Khan died in 1960's, who was very poor and absolutely illiterate and could hardly think of associating himself to Peer Ali Khan to gain the status of Freedom Fighter related family, even after the Independence of the country in 1947, no one came up to help the family, inspite of the fact that he was sent to gallows for espousing "patriotism" and not for any criminal offence. The said draconian law in fact was re-introduced after the independence with different names such as, TADA and Pota etc. and is being used extensively against Muslims in this free and republic of India.

It is a matter of sorrow and shame that we Indians specially Muslim historians dumped such selfless freedom fighters, "MUJAHIDS" who were responsible to wage "JEHAD" against British rule for the Independence of the Mother India and not for any personal gains or power. Peer Ali Khan and thousands of such brave men mostly Muslims entrusted their lives for the cause. The Britishers then and now are busy in their efforts to call such selfless Mujahids as fanatics etc. and now calls them Terrorist and such other derogatory names and our print as well as Electronic media gives such false perceptions publicity. J.M. Lewis the then D.M. of Patna in his letter dated 11.07.1857 wrote to the British Government that the "brave men with Peer Ali Khan were Saiyed Lootf Ali Khan the richest banker of Patna City and Maulvi Ali Kareem an astitute organizer." Such observation are not published. Other supporters who were working with Peer Ali Khan including Waris Ali an officer in British army with the rank of Jamadar attached to Trihut and Danapur cantonment were hanged on 5th July or earlier. Waris Ali was actively organizing revolt in the native Army personnel at Danapur cantonment. Peer Ali Khan in fact had planned the attack on British establishments in Patna division with the help of his followers and then, the Danapur soldiers were to join him. Unfortunately Waris Ali, was a loud mouth man and openly boosted his intention with people. This exposed him and his activities premature and was arrested on 23rd June, 1857 with the help of William Robertson a rich Neel dealer. At the time of his arrest he was in the midst of writing a letter to the Zameendar of Dausi, Maulvi Ali Kareem. Mr. Robertson took in his possession the half written letter and read it. General Lloyed was commanding the Sikh Army at Danapur, and found out that Waris Ali was instigating the Sikhs to revolt. In one of the letters captured from Waris Ali the name of Peer Ali Khan was also mentioned thus it was for the first time after the arrest of Waris Ali the name of Peer Ali Khan came in the knowledge of William Taylor. But very few knew, who was this person Peer Ali Khan. He was working absolutely in a closed door method as against Waris Ali who was very loud mouth and used to talk of Revolt even where it was not necessary. That is why his activities got exposed and in turn he exposed Peer Ali Khan and his secret movement. According to Shad Azeemabadi in his book "Peer Ali" at page 24:

"Iss zamaney men William Taylor Patna ka Commissioner
(In those days William Taylor was the Commissioner of Patna.......

Tha.....woh tamam khufia karvaiyun se wakfiat rakhta tha,
He was aware of all the secret activities of the people.

uske pesh nazar Khwaja Hussain Ali Khan ka muquadma bhi
He also had at the background of his mind the case of Khwaja.

tha jis per subse pahle ilzame-baghwat aayad hua.
Hussain Ali, who was 1st to be accused of revolt.

Commissioner yeh bhi janta tha ki khas Patna ke under
The Commissioner was also aware that in Patna the Wahabi.

Wahabi mazhab ke log jehadi hain. Aisa na ho ki un logon ki
Sect People were Jehadies. He was apprehensive of secret.

taraf se koi saman-e-jehad ho raha ho ya sarkar ke khilaf koi
Jahadi activities from them against the Government.

sazish Kare? Peer Ali ek kitabfarosh tha iss liye uski logon ki
Peer Ali being merely book seller, was not

nigah men koi haisiyat na thi. Commissioner iss quisim ke
considered of any worth the status in their eyes. There was no reason.

mamooli logon se kis tarah waquif hota. Hatta ki Haji
for the Commissioner to know such ordinary people.

Ahmadullah Wahabiyon ke sardar bhee Peer Ali ko sirf ek
Even Haji Ahmadullah the leader of Wahabee Sect knew

kutabfarosh ki haisiyat se jante thee."
Peer Ali merely a book seller.)

At p. 400, G.W. Forrest quoted Taylor:

> "Wahabees, a Sect of Mohammedan fanatics whose founder, Saiyed Ahmed, had fifty years before formed a permanent Center at Patna."

At page 233 of the Book "Memoirs of William Taylor, Taylor has shown his feelings of Anti Wahabee or for that matter anti-Muslims:

The notorious Wahabee Traitor Maulvi Ahmad Oolla and p. 231, while justifying his actions describing the reasons of Mr. Samuel, who replaced Mr. Taylor as Commissioner of Patna division after the revolt on 03.07.1857, becoming anti-Taylor was because: "intensified by the addition of a Mohammedan law officer as an assistant to the new Commissioner."

Charles Allen, p. 146 of his book "The God's Terrorist", writes:

> "A serious breach had now opened between Taylor and the Collector of Patna, Mr. Woodcock on the one hand, and the sessions Judge Mr. Farquharson and the two magistrates Mr. Lewis and Mr. Elliat on the other."

> "The first Party felt that the second were failing in their duties to uphold the law and were showing marked signs of pusillanimity, while the second considered that Taylor had cut too many judicial corners in arresting and sentencing on the basis of suspicion rather than proof."

> "Furthermore, Taylor had acted without proper consultation with Calcutta and in some instances against the advice of his colleagues, so providing further ammunition for his critics. Both in Calcutta and in Patna Taylor's enemies were already working to bring about his downfall."

Mr. G.W. Forrest in his book Volume III, p. 401 has quoted Tailor on his decision to arrest the Wahabee leaders, on or about 19/ 25.06.1857 as to why he arrested them and what he thinks about them:

> "I am not aware whether the Lt. Governor is well acquainted with the characteristics of the Wahabees, and it would take time to fully detail them; but I may observe, that one of the most remarkable features in their Sect is the fanatical devotion of the followers to their spiritual heads; this abnegation of self, and unquestioning submission to their religious leaders combined with great numbers of the Sect, is what renders them dangerous. There is such a perfect understanding between them that little or no written correspondence is necessary; a message could be verbally communicated from Patna to all the neighbouring districts without a letter being written, and this with little chance of detection or legal proof; for their fidelity to one another is as remarkable as their subordination to their spiritual leaders. That in the event of any more serious crisis, and any eminent successor being obtained against us, these Wahabees would be ready to merge their own differences with other Mussalmans, and join in a crusade against the English, I have little doubt, but that there had been secret gathering, among them of late, I had ample information."

The following passage from Book "A History of Indian Mutiny" Vol. 1 by W.G. Forrest, p. 484 shows how much biased the Britishers were against the Muslims:

> "Lieutenant Bogle in an attempt to penetrate into a house filled with desperate fanatics of the Mussalman faith was

badly wounded. The village was set on fire, but still the terrible fight continued. It was sad, very sad, to see our men pulled out, so to speak, dead and dying from the entrance of the houses they were trying in detail to storm."

If the British Army was trying to enter the houses of the Muslims in a village near Unnao and the entire village was burnt, in that situation what the Britishers expected from the Muslims, to welcome them? If Britishers were resisted in self-defence by Muslims and in the process some of them killed they describe Muslims as "fanatics".

G.W. Forrest further, pp. 405-07, writes:

On 2nd July, 1857, the Commissioner of Patna wrote to the Lt. Governor in regard to his measures, pertaining to the security submissions of the town (Patna):

"............ matters will be carried by us with a high hand, and that it behooves all the Company's subjects, not only not to conspire against the State or insult its officers, but to show, by a submission and respectful demeanour, that they recognize and fear the constituted authorities. I hope I am not asking much in begging to be allowed to judge of such matters from my local experience and observation."

Taylor an employee of Trading Company, calls Indians as "Company's Subject" and that he claimed right of subjugation of Indians to him.

"On the evening of the following day i.e. 3rd July, 1857 there was a riot in the town reduced to (entire submissiveness according to a plan) says Taylor (which appeared to have been concerted some few days previously, issued into the streets with two large flags and a drum beating; the cry of (Ali ! Ali ! Deen!) was immediately raised; and the party proceeded at once to the Roman Catholic mission house, with the declared intention of murdering the priest. He, however, had fortunately escaped before their arrival; and they left the house reiterating their cries, and calling on the people to join them."

> "Dr. R. Lloyal, assistant to the opium agent ordered fifty of the Nujeebs (Semi trained Native police) to lead and follow him, and, accompanied by eight Sikhs, he hastened to the scene of tumult. On approaching the rioters he rode forward to expostulate with them. He was shot dead from his horse, and before any man could come to his rescue some wretches rushed forward and hacked his face with their swords."

What a way to expostulate (persuade not to do) fully armed and accompanied by Police force?

The intelligence and secrecy with which Peer Ali Khan was working. That even his close associates, except few, were in dark about the real plan of Peer Ali Khan. It was only after his arrest and execution the real Peer Ali Khan came to be known as the leader of Revolutionaries. The secrecy in which Peer Ali Khan was working and the way he kept in secret his relations with Nawab Mir Abdullah and his son Nawab Lootf Ali while remaining in Patna itself shows the great organizational abilities of Peer Ali Khan. There were two persons with the name of Ghaseeta in the group of Peer Ali Khan. Both of them had been ex-employees of Saiyed Lootf Ali Khan, who were the messengers between Peer Ali Khan and Lootf Ali Khan. One out of the two Ghaseeta's mother was in fact working as Aya of the mother of Lootf Ali Khan who were the link between Peer Ali and Lootf Ali. This way Peer Ali Khan avoided direct link with his mentors Nawab Mir Abdullah and Lootf Ali Khan.

Taylor's "Thirty-eight Years in India," p. 524, quotes "Mallesons":

> "Amongst these were Peer Ali, the actual leader, and Shekh Ghaseeta, the confidential servant of Lootf Ali Khan, the richest banker of the city. It was clearly proved that Peer Ali was a main agent for promoting a crusade against the English: and for months he and the Shekḥ Ghaseeta had engaged and kept in pay numerous men who should be ready when called upon, to fight Peer Ali was poor. His associate Ghaseeta, was the hand of the great banker."

Saiyed Lootf Ali Khan was arrested by William Taylor on 5th July, 1857 in the night and was put to trial by Taylor before himself. He did not realize that his absolute authority both as prosecutor and Judge will be withdrawn soon. Mir Abdullah acted faster than Taylor could realize. If he would have had even the slightest inclination of what was going to happen the very next day, he would have hanged both Peer Ali Khan and Saiyed Lootf Ali Khan on 05.07.1957 itself. Though he got Peer Ali hanged on 7th July 1857 but some how the hanging of Saiyed Lootf Ali was stalled and in the mean time the Governor-General transferred the trial of Lootf Ali Khan to the regular session court of Mr. R.N. Farquharson the session judge of Patna hence the power of judge as well as prosecutor which Taylor had self-acquired was no more available to him and the trial of Saiyed Lootf Ali was transferred to the said session judge who inspite of best efforts of Taylor held Saiyed Lootf Ali not guilty and ordered for his release. A book with the title of "Trial of Lootf Ali Khan" is available in Khuda Baksh Oriental Library Patna.

5

The Narrative by T.R.E. Holmes and G.B. Mallesons

The book, History of the Indian Mutiny by T.R.E. Homes, p. 185 records as under:

> "On the 3rd July, a riot broke out in Patna itself. However, the bulk of the malcontents had been too thoroughly frightened by Taylor's measures to join it, it was easily suppressed by the Sikhs, while the ringleaders were seized and brought to trial. Chief among them was a Mohammedan book-seller named Peer Ali. A number of letters having been found in the house of a single man, were intently a mere sample of others, that Peer Ali would never have kept men in his pay except for a regular plot, and that Waris Ali had been ready to give up his lucrative situation in order to join Ali Kareem's enterprise. Taylor argued the existence of an extensive conspiracy, which, his own anticipatory, measures and had alone prevented from issuing in an appalling calamity. Peer Ali himself bore the most emphatic Testimony to Taylor's vigilance by conferring that his strong measures had forced the conspirators to strike on 3rd July, 1857 before they were ready. As per Peer Ali's pleadings the revolt was to start after Danapur army had revolted but Waris Ali's arrest disturbed the programme. They and twenty-one of their associates, convicted of having taken part in riot, were summarily hanged."

In another memoir known as "Parl Papers" Vol (xliv), Part-II pp. 6-13 and 15-23 and in Patna crisis pp. 65-72, it is stated that the Peer Ali's planning was not part of Wahabi movement but it was absolutely independent, which says:

> "It is important to notice that this was not a Wahabi plot. The Wahabis were now powerless. Peer Ali was a native of Lucknow, and had been corresponding treasonably with one Museeh-ooz-Zaman of Lucknow ever since the annexation of Oudh."

The Oudh annexation proclamation was issued on 7th February, 1856.

G.B. Mallesons in his book, "The Indian Mutiny of 1857" published in 1894 by Seeley and Co. Ltd. Esex Street, Strand, London 5th Edition reprinted in New Delhi in 2006 described Maulvi Ahmadullah, p. 17 as under:

> "A Tall, lean, muscular, with large deep-set eyes, beetle brows, a high equiline nose and lantern Jaws."

He further quotes Sir Thomson Seaton, p. 17:

> "As a man of great abilities, of undaunted courage of stern determination and by for the best soldier among the rebels."

Malleson, pp. 17-18 and 27 gives the following description of Maulvi which shows his Nationalist character:

> "Soon after the annexation of Oudh he travelled over the North West Province on a mission which was a mystery to the European authorities. He stayed in Delhi, Mirath (Meerut) Agra, Patna and Calcutta. Shortly after his return (to Faizabad) in April, 1857, he circulated seditious papers throughout Oudh. The (British) executives at Lakhnao (Lucknow) were alarmed and dispatched a body of troops to seize him. He was taken prisoner (in Faizabad) tried and condemned to death. Before the sentence could be executed the Mutiny broke out and he escaped. Thereafter, he became the confidential friend of the Begham of Lakhnao and trusted leader of the rebels. He

also devised the famous, 'Chapati Scheme' for communication of his message. I have already referred to the action of the Maulvi of Faizabad as being instrumental in creating and increasing the under current of hostility to British rule throughout Bengal to North-West Provinces."

Museeh-ooz-Zaman an associate of Maulvi Ahmadullah Madrasi and Begum Hazrat Mahal was the main person with whom Peer Ali Khan was in constant touch. After his hanging many letters and papers found in the shop of Peer Ali Khan which established his link to Maseeh-ooz-Zaman.

This appears to be the main reason Peer Ali Khan was thought to be native of Lucknow and the name village Mohammedpur and Azamgarh did not come or was kept away from the knowledge of William Taylor thus the village and its people escaped the total destruction.

6

The Conditions Prevalent in Patna Division During 1845-57 as Narrated by those Who were Present in Patna at that Time and the Corruption Prevalent Among the East Indian Company Employees

At the end of 1845 AD the Government of East India Company became aware of the conspiracy that Danapur's native army was being instigated by certain elements against the British. Britishers gave due importance to this information. G.B. Mollesons writes:

> "In 1845 a group of conspirators were busy to generate revolt in Patna. They were distributing cash to native armed men. One document was captured, which contained the names of about 100 prominent families. It also contained the names of certain important people of Patna, such as Welayat Ali (this Welayat Ali is a different person from Saiyed Welayat Ali Khan the grandson Mir Abdullah) and Enayat Ali the deputies of Saiyed Ahmed. (Ref. p. 208, "Hindustan's Wahabee Tehreek)

William Taylor, the Commissioner of Patna wrote:

> "For the last many years Patna was being considered as the center of conspiracy and angry people. In 1846 one very dangerous conspiracy was discovered, in which many Muslims of Patna and its surroundings were found involved. In the conspiracy efforts were made to instigate the native soldiers to revolt. The 1846 conspiracy was

> considered a very big conspiracy by all knowledgeable persons of this country. The object of the conspiracy was to destroy the British and to remove the British Government and re-establish the rule of Muslims."

W. Hunter while narrating the happening of 1852 wrote:

> "During same period Patna Magistrate reported that number of Revolutionaries/Mutineers and such organization are increasing in the city (Patna) and the revolutionaries of the capital of British capital are openly preaching revolt. Even police was also supporting these crazy people, and out of these one had collected at his house 700 people for this very purpose for this purpose so that they should be able to fight if Government take any step against it."

T.R.E. Holmes, G.W. Forrest, John Kaye, G.B. Malleson and other British historians are all praise for Taylor the way he was able to crush the rebellion in Patna Division. According to T.R.E. Holmes and others Taylor should not have been removed from his post nor he should have been accused by his superiors of cruelty against Indians. In support Malleson says that, "Taylor was responsible for the lives of some hundreds of Europeans scattered all over the province, a treasury in his own city, containing more than £ 3,00,000 and in the districts of still more for opium of the value of millions for his own good name and for the credit and honour of his country."

According to Malleson and other British historians it was justifiable to indiscriminately kill Indians to save few hundred or thousand Britishers and the ill-gotten wealth these Britishers accumulated from Indians.

T.R.E. Holmes also writes, pp. 203-04 of his book, "A History of Indian Mutiny":

> "The whole of Patna was nearly ship wrecked, at the moment when the rebels rose at Danapur, and before that, when the mischievous mechanization of Peer Ali Khan was such that, had it not been, Waris Ali's over enthusiastic

burst in Danapur before the Peer Ali scheme of revolt by the British Army of Indian soldiers followed by the people of Patna and Bihar including Wahabis, could take shape the British rule in Patna division would have been wiped out. Because of Waris Ali's arrest and seizure of letters which contained the names of Peer Ali, Ali Kareem and various others the entire plot got exposed before it could take place. Peer Ali Khan was left with no option but to advance his programme and revolted with his followers on 3rd July, 1857 even before the soldiers of Danapur could revolt. Dr. Lloyal was killed and Peer Ali and his followers were arrested. Those close to Peer Ali Khan were hanged at the bank Ganga and those who were found having sympathy with Peer Ali Khan were sentenced for life and were sent to Andaman and Nikobar Island as condemned prisoners and died."

What a justification to indiscriminate killing of Indians to save the so-called honour of his Country?

At this point it is necessary to mention that Saiyed Lootf Ali Khan, the richest banker of Patna helped Peer Ali Khan financially. Lootf Ali also grew with him under the guidance of his father Mir Abdullah. But inspite of all torture and allurements from Taylor, Peer Ali Khan did not disclose the name of Saiyed Lootf Ali Khan and others even when he was offered amnesty of his life by Taylor, Peer Ali Khan took the gallows on 7th July, 1857, cool and defiant. However, Lootf Ali Khan remained under arrest. J.M. Lewis the D.M. of Patna in his letter of 11th July, 1857 wrote to the Government of East India Company i.e., the Governor-General Sir George Canning who was personal friends of Mir Abdullah the father of Saiyed Lootf Ali:

"At the request of the Commissioner Mr. Taylor, I arrested him (Lootf Ali Khan) on the night of 5th instant. I was accompanied by Lt. Compbel with guards of Sikhs who surrounded the house but the precaution was needless, as there was no show of resistance or attempt to escape. He at once came out to meet me and when informed that he had been summand by the Commissioner, he ordered his carriage and as the coachman was not forthcoming, got himself on the base, and drove us to Taylor's house. The commissioner there informed him that he was a prisoner, and ordered me to take him at once to the Civil Jail, but as no preparations had been made for his reception, as it was past 1 O'clock, I obtained permission from the Commissioner to take him to my own house where I gave him a room and the next morning he was lodged in the Meethapur Jail. In fact, there was no ground for his detention."

"Saiyed Lootf Ali Khan, however, proved a hard nut to crack. Taylor sought obsessively to prosecute this famous banker so as to have him hanged, but the Session Judge of Patna, R.N. Farquharson, frustrated the Wily Commissioner (Taylor)."

"Taylor made several attempts to influence the Session Judge to bend the judicial process and hang Lootf Ali. But the Judge did not succumb. Taylor even complained against the Judge Farquharson but his pleas were not accepted. Contrarily, Taylor was sacked from his job, his loyalty to Crown not withstanding."

(Also A.K. Biswas and I.K. Shukla)

Taylor had charged Lootf Ali of harbouring a mutineer of the army who was hanged sometimes in June 1857. Lootf Ali was also charged for harbouring a leading rebel, Shekh Ghaseeta a close associate of Peer Ali who was also hanged along with other associates of Peer Ali. Shekh Ghaseeta was an old employee of Lootf Ali and was actively associated and involved with Peer Ali Khan in his pursuit of generating the revolt specially in the night of 3rd July, 1857 when Dr. Lloyel was killed. Another "hardened rebel" whose name was also Ghaseeta who along with his mother were also the employees of Lootf Ali. The mother of Shekh Ghaseeta who was the "Aaya" of Lootf Ali's mother was also active member of Peer Ali Khan's team. Besides the above one Mohbbat Ali Khan or Mohile Ali a rebel sepoy, who took part in the revolt of the 37th Regiment N.I. at Bananas on or about 4th June, 1857 also took shelter at Lootf Ali's house; and was arrested and hanged.

Inspite all the above evidence and Taylor's pressure and persistent efforts to get Saiyed Lootf Ali Khan sentenced to death the Judge acquitted Lootf Ali and released him. This would have been difficult had Peer Ali Khan, disclosed his connection with Saiyed Lootf Ali Khan and his father Mir Abdullah. This shows the strong character and gratefulness of Peer Ali Khan towards his mentor. A true Pathan.

It will not be out of place to mention that at the time Peer Ali Khan was arrested and hanged along with his associates there was no effective judicial system and Taylor was working like an autocrat. However, just to show that justice was done and as a face saving device an army court, for name sake, was established by Taylor comprising of General Lloyd and Major Rettrey, William Taylor himself. But the main actor in this summery trial was William Taylor who ordered to hang, Peer Ali Khan and his followers, General Lloyd and Major Rettery just put their signatures.

Sir George Canning as well as James Fredrick Halliday the Lft. Governor knew that so long Taylor was at the helm of Patna Division he will not spare Lootf Ali. Hence in August, 1857, i.e. the very next month after hanging of Peer Ali Khan William Taylor alongwith Maula Baksh were sacked as Commissioner and Deputy Commissioner of Patna division and enquiry was instituted against Taylor. It was only because of the proceedings against Taylor and his removal and enquiry, immediately after 7th July, 1857 and taking over by Mr. Samuel as Commissioner of Patna division and the friendship of Mir Abdullah with Sir George Canning and the Lft. Governor of Bengal and the money power of Mir Abdullah the enquires about Peer Ali Khan was dropped after his hanging to avoid detection of his linkage with Lootf Ali. Taylor was shunted out of Patna and sent to Dhaka. Due to his removal Taylor was not able to go deep into the affairs of Peer Ali Khan hence the native place of Peer Ali Khan, village: Mohammedpur also could not be linked with him. Thus not only his brother Nasrullah Khan and his family but the entire village Mohammedpur escaped from being destroyed and people from being killed by the cruel Taylor as per his order referred to above.

Dr. Moti Chand, Director, Prince of Wales Museum, Bombay in his book "Kashi Ka Itihas" published in September, 1962 has described, pp. 250-75, the details of bribes offered/demanded and given by the rulers of Banaras Raja Balwant Singh and his son Chet Singh. to the British Governors and British Residents (Chet Singh was the son of Balwant Singh from his *Rakhel* Panna Devi). This shows that the employees of East India Company were very found of bribes and were corrupt. Those Indians who had the money could get their work done by paying the bribe but the common people who could hardly afford two meals a day suffered.

Dr. Moti Chand in his book, p. 264, mentions:

> "In 1766, Balwant Singh succeeded in getting the Patta of Banaras in his favour and out of the domain of Nawab of Oudh, by bribing Rs. 8 lac in cash as well as in kind in the shape of certain territory to spencer the local resident of East India Company. Immediately thereafter Balwant confiscated all the "Mafees Land" given to Muslims by the Nawab of Oudh. The Muslims complained to British Mariat. Balwant restored some of the Mafees so long Mariat was present in Banaras but no sooner he left Balwant again confiscated it."

Further, pp. 380-82, Dr. Moti Chand says:

> "In 1857 revolt, Banaras became a very important Military Center of the Britishers which helped them in transit, supply and movement of troops through the Grand Trunk Road to Northern and Western India.

Period of Lord Clive was full of corruption. Clive himself was very corrupt hence the Employees of East India Company also became very corrupt.

Clive had settled to pay Seth Ami Chand a very rich businessman of Bengal a sum of Rs. 30 lac in return of obtaining his support and help to oust Sirajuddaula. After Sirajuddaula was defeated and killed Clive became dishonest and did not pay the amount to Seth Ami Chand and suddenly Seth Ami Chand died mysteriously. Clive had amassed lot of wealth through all kinds of ways fair and foul, through conspiracy and intrigues. He collected huge amount from Mir Jaffar. Through conspiracy Clive also obtained from Moghal King Shah Alam contract to collect Land Revenue from Bengal, Bihar and Orissa and agreed to pay Rs.30 crore to Shah Alam annually. Thus, he took full powers over the Zameendars as well as Land tillers. He fully exploited this power to amass wealth for himself and made the life of common men as hell.

Clive was recalled to England in 1767 but was shocked, when reached to England and found that the English Press, the Parliament and people of England were hostile to him.

He lived in England after his return luxuriously in his newly purchased comfortable houses acquired out of the millions of Rupees, plundered from India through bribes and frauds but he died only as a disgraced and a very unhappy person even from his own family (Ref. *The National Herald,* Daily New Delhi dt. 29.07.2006).

Clive was replaced by John Cartier. But he was also equally corrupt but not as bold and cunning like Clive. He accepted to take the bribe of Rs.10 lac from Sirajuddaula to refuse Balwant the ruler of Banaras an independent status. But Balwant managed through the local resident to pay the said 10 lac to Cartier and paid Rs. 1 lac to the local resident and placed his head and Turban on the feet of Cartier and promised greater loyalties to British. Cartier changed his side from Sirajuddaula to Balwant and made him almost independent out of Oudh and under East India Company directly.

(Ref. "Kashi Ka Itihas" by Dr. Moti Chand)

William Taylor himself records in his Memoirs reproduced by Mr. Chaturbhuj, p. 137 as to how the officials of East India Company amassed wealth for themselves:

> There was also old gentleman of the name of John Bardeo Elliot, a retired civilian who had been for some years employed as special Commissioner in the province, where he had amassed a large fortunes, and on resigning the

> service remained at 'Patna as a permanent resident, purchasing a house, with a beautiful garden, surrounded on all side by a high wall. The collector of the district was Mr. Anson."

According to Taylor this Bardeo Elliot was of very loose character and has kept many native women in his villa. Hence when Taylor's wife came to join him in Patna Taylor did not allow her to visit his villa and the opinion of Taylor about Elliot came to the knowledge of Elliot. Since that time Bardeo Elliot became enemy number one of Taylor and played a significant role in the ouster of Taylor.

7

Peer Ali Khan, Teepu Sultan their Bold Posture for Nationalism Undermined Malafidely

A.K. Biswas wrote: The sadistic, savagery and brutal (killing) and illegality of destruction of property distinguished William Taylor.

Peer Ali Khan on surface was merely a book-seller of Patna. But that wont described him fairly.

Peer Ali and his friend had risen against the British in Patna before the revolt broke out in Shahabad, Gaya or Danapur Cantonment. This cost them dearly. He, however, must be the 1st and only book-seller under the Sun to have been sent to the gallows for espousing patriotism. Destiny ordained that Peer Ali set a very high moral tone and stiff standards for martyrs in modern India."

After executing Peer Ali on 7th July, 1857 Taylor recorded rather faithfully the last words of this dauntless son of Mohammedpur Azamgarh (A.K. Biswas called him daunted son of Patna). In his letter of July 8, 1857 to James Frederick Halliday, the Lt. Governor of Bengal,Taylor quoted the words of Peer Ali Khan, on his offer of Pordorn in return of Peer Ali Khan disclosing the names of all those who were associated with him, Peer Ali said:

> "There are some occasions on which it is good to give up life and that, if I, sacrificed, thousand others, everyday, would fill their place."

These were the last words uttered by Peer Ali Khan just before he was hanged on 7th July, 1857. Udham Singh who was hanged in Pentonville Prison of London for killing the Ex. Punjab Governor Michael O'Dwyer for his crimes in Jalianwala Bagh on April 13, 1919 said just before his hanging:

> "I don't care about the sentence of death. It means nothing at all. I am dying for a purpose. We are suffering from British empire..... I am proud to die to free my native land, and hope that when I am gone, in my place will come thousand of my countrymen to drive you, dirty dogs out.......... You will be cleaned out of India."

A.K. Biswas says that, "Khudiram Bose, Bhagat Singh, Raj Guru, Sukhdeo and Udham Singh—one and all-during India's freedom struggle courted death with exactly the words of Peer Ali had uttered in 1857." These words of Udham Singh is given wide publicity by one and all with pride, *rightly so*, but how many know that the originator of these sentiments and words was Peer Ali Khan who said it on 7th July, 1857 on the gallows i.e. 83 years 24 days prior to 31st July, 1940. They were merely repeated by Udham Singh. Our historians are guilty of suppressing the extreme sacrifice of Peer Ali Khan and his brave words on the Gallows. His selfless sacrifice for the nation should not have been under played as has been done.

Similarly, the credit for the origin of "Swadeshi Movement" and "Non-Co-operation Movement" started in 20th century is made to believe that it's originator was Mahatma Gandhi. But how many people of India or World know that it was Teepu Sultan, who started it, about 135 years before Gandhiji's adoption of such movement.

Teepu Sultan after settling as ruler as a first step ordered that all sorts of economic relationship with Britishers be stopped. No one should keep any business relationship with Britishers. No goods imported and/or manufactured by Britishers will be purchased by anyone nor the native people will sell any goods to them.

Teepu himself practiced it by completely discarding throughout his life, the use of foreign goods and cloths. Teepu even forbidden the sale and/ or purchase of salt manufactured in Madras, because Madras was under the control of Britishers. Some Bangalore traders once purchased salt from Madrass. Teepu made the Bangalore traders not to sell the said salt in his state and made them to return it to Madras traders.

Teepu was so strong in his character that when one of his officers Frasat Khwaja sent a list of medicine for him suggested by Hakeem Mohammed Beg, Teepu wrote back on 21.12.1785 to Etamdee that his list of Medicines contains some essence of European countries, which he will not use. He directed Etemadee to consult with Hakeem Mohammed Beg to suggest some alternative Unani Medicine in place of European medicines. (Saheefa Teepu Sultan, p. 276, letter no. 183, "Tehreeke Azadi Men Ulema Ka Kirdar, p. 211).

Teepu never slept on bed but used to sleep on thick khaddar on the ground. No historian gave the credit to Teepu and made it only a programme of Mahatma Gandhi who only followed the method adopted by Teepu Sultan. Only one person Sardar Kant Raj Urs, Ex. Deewan of Mysore State wrote in October, 1919 issue of "Maithic Society Journal, p. 35:

> "What is known today the Swadeshi Movement" it's founder was Teepu Sultan and its object was by Teepu to save India from foreign dependence."

But how many people know it? Because our media and historians did not want to write the Truth because Teepu was a Muslim.

The above details are quoted in the Book, "Tehreeke Azadi Men Ulema Ka Kirdar", pp. 191-212, source from "Saheefa Teepu Sultan", p. 276, letter numbers 183 and 430, 183. The above important aspect of Teepu Sultan's life are also not only under played but there are many fanatics who tried to project, Teepu as anti-Hindu and not a patriot and Muslim historians are silent. What a Shame?

Taylor the killer of Shaheed-e-Azam, Peer Ali Khan wrote to the Governor Bengal in his letter dated 8th July, 1857 that at the time Peer Ali was being taken to the Gallows:

> "He was cool and defiant to the last, though manacled and wounded, and with the sentence over him, he showed neither fear, nervousness, nor shame. In character, appearance, and manners, he was the perfect ideal of a brutal and brave fanatic."

(A.K. Biswas and I.K. Shukla)

These are words of William Taylor himself to describe Peer Ali Khan. What a shame, our historians specially Muslim historians did not find any place or courage to write about Peer Ali Khan among the martyrs of the country. Was it not because he was not from any celebrity family or any rich man, he was a poor man and a Muslim?

Shad Azeemabadi in his book "Peer Ali", p. 8 has written that on 2nd July, 1857 the entire population of Patna were agog with conflicting news. Every where people in group of three and four were discussing in hush voices. The city shops were half closed/ half open. Shops were closed early in the evening. Peer Ali's shop was just adjacent and on the Western side of Padri's Haveli. Adjacent to the same the *haweli* (Kothi) of Saiyed Welayat Ali Khan, son of Saiyed Mehdi Ali and grand son of Mir Abdullah and nephew of Lootf Ali, was situated.

Welayat Ali just to remain in the good books of Britishers was always eager to collect information of the City and its native population and their activities and used to pass on the same to British officials. He was working more as their informer. The British Government bestowed upon Welayat Ali with Jageer and Khetabs highest of them was "Order of the Indian Empire" for the services he rendered to Britishers.

Immediately after the arrest of Waris Ali, William Taylor with the help of Deputy Collector Maula Baksh had already confiscated all the Guns from the people of Patna, Azeemabad and surroundings, and had promulgated Sec.144 in the City.

Still with the secret help of one Maulvi Medhi the patrolling Magistrate of city of Patna few guns reached possession of Peer Ali Khan. Later Maulvi Medhi was arrested on 20th June, 1857 and was prosecuted by Taylor for dereliction of duty. Fortunately, Taylor could not get the information of the guns reaching in the hands of Peer Ali.

All the Zameendars whether Hindu or Muslim were supporters of English Government, because with the help of Britishers they had by force captured and occupied the land of poor peasants. These Zameendars exploited and looted the Poor Peasants and in the process they were filling their own as well as Britishers pockets. No one was there to help the poor masses, there was complete anarchy. These Zameendars knew that their interest was with the British. Mr. A.K. Biswas has rightly stated that, feudal Lords, Zamindars, Talookdars, *thikadars* and even intelligentsia with no shame or embarrassment, flaunted their loyalty to beastly British aliens. Arrayed against their country and fellow nationals.

8

Maulana Fazle Haque Khairabadi and His Narration of the Events of 1857 Karl Marx and His Narration of the Events of 1587

In the book "Baghi-e-Hindustan", p. 408 onwards the conditions prevalent prior to 1857 as was recorded by Maulana Fazle Haque Khairabadi in brief was as under:

> "In the country Hindus or Muslims were comprising of Agriculturists, peasants business men, crafts men and daily-wage workers. In Delhi majority was of Muslims with negligible Hindus. So long Kings and Rajas were ruling people did not have any problem for their day-to-day living, because people had various options of employment in Armed forces, Government jobs, besides agriculture, handicrafts etc. Almost everyone was engaged in one or the other job or employment.
>
> However, since the Britisher got themselves involved practically in every walk of life, the problem of unemployment, increased alarmingly, practically everyone is in financial mess poor are suffering due to hunger.
>
> Britishers have taken total control of the Business. They are importing practically everything from their country including cloths, foodgrains and all other merchandise and selling it here thus destroying the local production units. They have confiscated illegally and against the solemn commitment made by them in 1803 and 1805 AD all

(Mafees) i.e. the free allotments of land by the King of Nawabs and Rajas.

The land revenue has been increased in such proportion that poor peasants are unable to pay.

To feed themselves lacs of people opted in the job of spinning thread by 'Charkha', spinning jute, ropes, and 'Chakki' to grind wheat etc. Even that has been taken away as the Britishers have installed 'Panchakkis' place to place which has taken away even these household jobs from the poor people."

Allama Fazle Haque asked Bahadur Shah Zafar the Moghal King:

"Kindly let the people of the Country know as to whom they should approach to earn their livelihood? Even the beggars do not know as to who is now in a position to give alms. The condition of the people in general is so alarming."

Karl Marx in his letter dated 10th June, 1853, published in New York Daily Tribune, issue dated 25.06.1853 recorded, pp. 15-16, described the condition of the country as follows:

"There cannot, however, remain any doubt but that the misery inflicted by the British on Hindustan is of an essentially different and infinitely more intensive kind than all Hindustan had to suffer before."

"England has broken down the entire framework of Indian society, without any symptoms of re-construction, yet appearing. This loss of his old world, with no gain of a new one, imparts a particular kind of melancholy to the present misery, and separates Hindustan, ruled by Britain, from all its ancient traditions, and from the whole of its past History."

The miserable condition and torture of the common man has been described by Karl Marx, pp. 72-74 of the book containing his letter dated 28.08.1857 published in New York Daily Tribune dated 17.09.1857 as under:

> "Further, this exhorting of money applies only to taking the public money, or facing a further contribution from Ryot for the officer to put into his own pocket. There is therefore, no legal means of punishment whatever for the employment of force in collecting the public revenue."

> "Lord Dalhousie himself wrote in September, 1855 to the Directors (Court of Directors of East India Co.) that he has long ceased to doubt that torture in one shape or the other is practiced by the lower subordinate in every British province. Universal existence of torture as a financial institution of British India is thus officially admitted, but the commission is made in such a manner as to shield the British Government itself. In fact, the conclusion arrived by the Madras Commission that the practice of torture is entirely the fault of lover Hindu officials, which European Servants of the Government had always, however, unsuccessfully, done their best to prevent."

The above is very conservative narration of the conditions of the people of the country during 1857 AD.

The Coffer of East India Company was empty because of rampart corruption among its employees and also because of over indulgence in recruitment of Army, not to maintain law and order, but for capturing the already disintegrated, Moghal Kingdom and its provinces. In an effort to collect funds the East India company, Government made (*Istemrari Bandobast*, 1793 A.D.) and confiscated large number of Zameendaris of the old Zameendars. Most of the old Zameendars effected were in heavy debts, as their sons inspite of having lost the Jageerdari or Zameendari were unable to change their life style and *Ayashees*.

The peasantry as well as the village Zameendars, made subject to ever rising tax burden under *Mahalwari* system since 1822. In *Mahalwari* system the settlement used to be only for twenty years that too the land-tax could be changed at any time even within twenty years. If one peasant or landlord failed to pay land-tax not only his but his neighbour's land would stand forfeited to the Government.

The peasants and poor were unable to decide as to who was really responsible for their misery. On paper the country was being ruled by Moghal King or their Subedars. In actual life their Nazims were ruling with no responsibility and then in the name of protector of Kings, Nawabs and Rajas the Britishers were unleashing cruelty. The common man was being looted by Native rulers as well as the Britishers alike.

At page 32 of Karl Marx book in his letter dated 22.07.1853 it is recorded:

> "The paramount power of Great Moghals was broken by the Moghal Viceroys. The Power of Viceroys was broken by the Marathas. The Power of Marathas was broken by Afghans. The Maratha feudal lords competed with the Afghans for hegemony (leadership) in India and in 1661 suffered a crushing defeat. Bled heavily by the struggle for supremacy in India and the internal strife of their feudal lords, the Maratha principalities fell prey to the East India Company, which subjugated than in the Maratha War of 1803-05. That while all were struggling against all, the British rushed in and was able to subdue then all. A country not only divided between Mohammedans and Hindus, but between tribe and tribe, between caste and caste. A society whose framework was based on a sort of equilibrium resulting from general repulsion and constitutional exclusiveness between all its members—such a country and such a society, were they not the predestined prey of conquest? If we knew nothing of the past History of Hindustan, would there not be the one great incontestable fact, that even at this moment India is held in English thralldom by an Indian army maintained at the cost of India?"

The Muslim intelligentsia out of common people, understood the game plan of Britishers behind the scene, and the weakness of Moghal King, Nawabs and Rajas as well as small time Jageerdars and Zameendars. Finding the rulers incapable and incompetent some of them started organizing the silent revolt to throw the Britishers out of the country. This group comprised of mostly

Muslims, many of them Ulema and Maulvis, in which some were concerned with the National considerations and few were loyal to Moghal Kings. As for those who were rich and closer to the Kings and Nawabs finding the days of these Kings and Nawabs, numbered, silently started conspiring with the Britishers against their own mentors, in obvious effort to retain their lavish life style and Ayashees, in the bargain.

As for Hindu population was concerned it comprised of three groups. One, the business community as well as Zameendars and Jageerdars. The second group were common High Cast Hindu population, comprising of Brahmins and Chatrees, Kayastas and Khattarees etc. The third group was of poor peasants and untouchables. The first group had changed their loyalty from Moghals to Britishers. The second group was indifferent and not concerned as to who will rule upon them so long they were not unduly taxed but were not willing to support the Muslim revolutionaries, fearing revival of Muslim rule as was being projected to them by Britishers. The third group had no say as they were directly under the second group and not connected with the Government.

9

The Arrival of Muslims in India Right from 837 AD and Through Moghal Period. Role of Akbar and Jehangir in Crushing the Afghan and Turk Settlers in India and Efforts of Teepu Sultan to Unite all the Rajas and Nawabs Against Britishers

In about 837 AD with the arrivals of Arabs in the areas of Sind and Punjab specially Multan Muslims started settling in these provinces. These included, Abbasis, Siddiquis, Faruquis, Usmanis, Asharis, Banu Asad, Banu Atibba, Sadat. Multan has been the capital of Muslim rulers even prior to the invasion of Subuktagheen and his son Mehmood Ghaznavi. But this group of Muslims mostly Shekh and Saiyeds from Arab and Persia were mostly traders. Those settled in India got busy in Agriculture also. Some of them remained involved in business between India and Arab and Persia.

It was after the invasion of Mehmood Ghaznavi that large number of Turks and Afghan's got access to the gigantic plans to the Eastern borders of the Kingdom of Kannoj which at times extended even upto Bihar. The rulers of Kannoj had become ally of Mehmood and were under his direct protection hence allowed the free settlement of Afghans and Turks in his kingdom upto Bihar. These settlers were always ready to fight if need be in favour and at the instance of Afghan and Turk rulers.

For all practical purposes these Afghans and Turk settlers made India as their permanent abode and considered India as their home land.

Karl Marx, p. 32 says:

> "Arabs, Turks, Tartars and Moghals who had successfully over run India soon became, Hinduised."

Here Karl Marx adopted the word "Hinduised" from the word Hindustan, he in fact meant, "Indianised" or became Indian in all sense, and treated themselves the Native of India. The use of word "Hinduised" by Karl Marx may not be misunderstood as becoming Hindu in religious sense as he meant "Indian National".

The Afghan and Turk settlers offered full resistance to the establishment of Moghals who wanted to uproot the Afghan/ Turk rulers from India. During the period of Feroze Shah Tughlok and then during Lodi period these Afghans and Turks developed very good rapport and relation with these Rajputs who had migrated from Rajputana to Eastern part of U.P. upto Bihar during the period Mehmood Ghaznavi's frequent attacks. Thus a large number of Pathan/ Afghan Marshal race out of Muslims, and Rajputs out of the migrated and re-settled Rajputs were available. But this situation existed, so long, Afghan rulers or for that matter Sultanate continued i.e. till Ibrahim Lodi and the brief 5 years rule of Sher Shah Suri.

The relations between Afghan and Turk Muslim population and the Hindu population flourished during Lodi period between 1451 AD and 1526 AD, 75 years i.e., between Behlool, Sikander and Ibrahim Lodi. During this period Afghans and those Rajputs who had settled in U.P. and Bihar had developed a very close relation and both jointly constituted a strong force to recon with. Sikander Lodi infact was the first Muslim ruler who made efforts to inculcate feeling of brotherhood between Muslims and Hindus. He in fact invited the Hindu population to join in the Government jobs. He first invited Brahmins to study Persian so as to be able to work in Government departments. But Brahmins refused on the ground that their job is to impart religious teachings to Hindu population. Thereafter Sikander invited Chattarees, who also refused saying that they are not fit for Revenue job as they are Marshal race and would like to join in Armed forces only. Then Sikander invited Vaishs who also refused saying that they are business community and will remain as such and are not fit for Government jobs. Ultimately Kayastas accepted the invitations and in a very short span of period perfected and acquired not only working knowledge of Persian language but many of them became scholars in Persian literature and were able to compete with Muslim Scholars. Thus with the encouragement of Sikander Lodi Kayastas captured large number of Government jobs in the revenue department which in the Moghal period followed by British Raj almost became Monopoly of Kayastas.

(Reference book – "Salateen Hind", Vol. I, p. 297 by Hakeem Mufti Intezamullah Snehbai Akbarabadi published by Nadvatul Musanfeen, Delhi, 2nd edition, October, 1966.

Moghals considered Afghans as their enemy no. 1. Accordingly Afghan settlements in India also did not like the Moghals. Babur, after capturing Chanderi and by defeating Rana Sangram, directed his attention towards Bihar to crush Afghans settled there and in Eastern part of U.P. In fact, Humayun was thrown out of India by Sher Shah Suri with the help of Afghan's who had settled in India. That is why after Humayun's re-capture of India with the help of Iran, after the death of Sher Shah Suri, the future Moghal Kings particularly Akbar and Jehangir adopted the policy of repressive action against Afghan populations in India, and appeasement of Rajputs and Brahmins. They crushed the Afghan population in all respect, as a Nation and made them economically very poor and had to concentrate to earn their day-to-day livelihood, out of agriculture.

In fact, Akbar did the maximum repressive acts against Afghan settlers in India. He stayed for over a year in Nizamabad a town in the District of Azamgarh and crushed all the Afghan populace in the Eastern part of India. Elders of Mohammedpur say that when Akbar was stationed in Nizamabad the villages populated by Afghans around Nizamabad had to destroy all the proof of their connections with Afghanistan. In fact in Mohammedpur many such proofs and evidences were dumped in a well situated at

Western end of the Qabristan (Graveyard) and the well was filled with mud. Its upper circular edge is still visible. Thereafter, between 1584-1598 AD Akbar established his capital in Lahore and attacked Afghanistan to crush the Afghans so that they may not help the Afghan population of India and revolt against Moghals.

The region between Chandwak the border between Varanasi and Azamgarh and upto Dohri Ghat in the North of Azamgarh was the main Centre of Afghan and Rajput settlements and had very strong bond between them. Moghals found difficult to control the area. Jahangir devised a novel method to break the nexus between these Afghan settlements and the Rajputs and carved an independent Jagir, and appointed a Rajput, Abhimanyu Singh Gautam as its ruler. This was done to give the Rajputs upper hand over Afghans and thus created rift between them. The capital of this Jagir was made in Mahanagar about 20 kms east of Mohammedpur village. This very Jageer later became the kingdom of Azamgarh under Azam Shah who was the son of future generation of Abhimanyu Singh Gautam. Abhimanyu Singh Gautam had embraced Islam and named himself as Daulat Khan. His Tomb is intact in Mahanagar even today. Azamgarh City came into being during Aurangzeb by Azamshah. The rulers of Azamgarh fought two/three wars with Aurangzeb and the Nawab of Oudh and Jaunpur. It become District Azamgarh during British rule.

The book "Baghi-e-Hindustan", p. 355, mentions:

> "Afghans were famous in India as able and brave soldiers. Afghans had settled in large parts of country and were able fighters. Large part of Oudh army was out of such Afghan settlements, Pathans. Nawab Ameer Khan and many of his officers, and supporters were Afghan. Almost entire Rohel Khand was full of Afghan migratory. In Rai Bareilly the native place of Saiyed Ahmed Shaheed the entire Jahanabad Mohallah was of Afghan Pathans."

G.B. Malleson, p. 31 of his book, "The Indian Mutiny of 1857" describes the revolutionary nature of the people of the region comprising of Azamgarh, Jaunpur, Gorakhpur etc. having maximum Afghan and Turk settlers plus Rajputs:

"Thomson who was responsible to rule Azamgarh, Jaunpur, Gorakhpur, along with Agra, Kanpur, and adjoining Districts throughout Bundelkhand, tried to introduce Western style of Land management (*Mahalwari* system) which created discontent among the Zameendars of the above districts.

This system was tried by Akbar in effort to consolidate and control the territory but found it more counter-productive and withdrew the scheme. This was more extensive in the areas now District of Azamgarh, Jaunpur and Gorakhpur where Akbar feared to tread Thomson rushed in. With the result land owners of Jaunpur, Azamgarh and Gorakhpur became hostile. Azamgarh was the first to display disaffection and virtually revolted on 3rd June, 1857 and the revolt continued for a long time festering sore in the British side. The situation became so alarming that Lord Canning shifted his headquarters from Calcutta to Allahabad and reached on 9th February, 1858 to have effective control of the region. Still the Districts of Azamgarh and Jaunpur remained turbulent for sometime more."

The book, "Last Moghal", p. 220 has quoted a document issued by Shahzada Firoz Shah as under:

"A document known as Azamgarh proclamation was wholly secular in tone, and is aimed at a broad base of different interest groups; indeed, it is the nearest thing produced during the uprising to a manifesto of national independence. Its opening sentence sets the tone, a cry to arms noting that 'both Hindus and Mohammedans' are being ruined under the tyranny and oppressions the infidel and treacherous English. Most of its space is given over the complaints that English have over-taxed the land owners, monopolized, all the posts of dignity and emolument in the civil and armed services, and put Indian artisans out of business by flooding the market with cheap British imports."

The author of this document was Prince Firoz Shah, who was probably a grandson of Zafar (Bahadur Shah Zafar), fought exclusively in Oudh and Lucknow, and never once came to Delhi in the course of uprising.

The repressive attitude of Moghals for over 2 to 3 hundred years against the Afghan settlements in India, diminished their Marshal abilities. The rest Mirzas, Shekhs, Saiyeds and Brahmins and Rajputs occupied major high positions in Moghal rule. Right from the Darbar of the King and Nawabs upto Nazims most of the functionaries were from Shia Sect. The Muslim populace out of Afghan and Turks were kept away from occupying important positions. Birbal, Todar Mall and such other Brahmins were inducted by Akbar as his main advisers. Since Humayun could return to India with the help of Iran he and after him Akbar placed in all top assignments such as Governors only Shia Sect who came from Iran alongwith Humayun. Even the Britishers were given permission to do business in India by Moghal King Jahangir from Ajmer fort. Kayastas who were inducted in revenue departments by Sikander Lodi were continued by Moghals in the revenue departments. The Rajputs who assured their full support to Moghals were engaged in high ranks of the Army. Raja Man Singh was appointed Governor of Bihar and Bengal by Akbar in an area thickly populated by Afghans. Even Raja Birbal was assigned to crush Yosufzais (Afghanis) and was killed in the process on 25th February, 1586. Afghans were deprived to occupy high positions and were left dependent only on agriculture. This was the strategy by Moghals to avoid any possible future revolt from Afghans to their empire.

The rulers of various states in Rajputana, with the aim and object to be in good book of Moghal Kings and to capture all plum posts in the Moghal Kingdom adopted the policy of appeasement to Moghal Kings. In this effort most of the Rajputana rulers offered their daughters as the Bride to the Moghal Kings. Akbar had five Rajput wives:

1. Jodha Bai (mother of Saleem/Jehangir) daughter of Raja Bahara Mall Kchwa—the rulers of Jaipur.
2. The daughter of Bekaner ruler Kalyan Mall,

3. Daughter of Raja Dangarpur,

4. Tara Bai as well as, and

5. Man Bahuti.

Similarly Jehangir also had five Rajput wives:

1. Jodha Bai alias Jagat Gosain (daughter of Raja Udai Singh. She was the mother of Khurram the Shahjahan). (On 30.01.2007 on Star T.V. in their programme K.B.C. they declared a wrong answer "Manmati" as correct.)

2. Daughter of Raja Bhagwan Dass who was titled by Jehangir "Shah Begum".

3. Daughter of Raja Kishore Dass Rathore.

4. Daughter of Raja Rai Singh Rawal.

5. Daughter of Bheem Wali of Jaisalmer.

Besides the above Hindu wives Jehangir also married Noor Jahan the ex-wife of Sher-e-Afghan, and another woman daughter of Khwaja Hasan named Saleh Jamal.

(Ref. "Salateen-e-Hind", Vol. II).

Shahjahan was involved in enjoying the kingdom established by Akbar and Jahangir and remained dependent on the Rajput and Irani advisers.

This pushed the Muslim population, majority being Afghans and Turks, economically weak. Aurangzeb was the grandson of Jodha Bai alias Jagat Gosain and great grandson of Jodha Bai daughter of Jaipur ruler, both Rajputs. Inspite of the fact that Aurangzeb was born in India, his grand and great grandmothers were Hindu Rajput still he is described as foreigner and his rule as foreign rule, by the fanatical Hindus.

Urdu Poet Quais Rampuri rightly described the situation as under:

Keya Sitam hai ki yaheen paida hue hum Phir bhi
(Even after having born on Indian soil–still !)

Maadre Hind ki aaghosh ke haqdar Naheen
(Not entitled to the lap of the Mother India)

Tum Agar raaz bhee becho to wafadar ho
(You claim to be loyal even if you sell the secrets of the Nations)

Hum agar ser bhee kata len to wafadar naheen
(Even if the sacrifice our life for the Nation we are accused not loyal.)

The fault of Aurangzeb, was that he tried to correct the damage and imbalance created by Akbar and Jahangir between Hindus and Muslims. He tried to create parity between all sections of population, whether Hindu or Muslims. He did not have the ego of being Moghal but an Indian and wanted all Indian, Hindus or Muslims to be at par. He also threw Britishers out of India and did not allow them to establish for many years. With the result the Indian historians including English historians such as H.M. Elliot termed him communal. Sir Jadavnath Sarkar, a British decorator with the title of "Sir" and Honorary member of Royal Asiatic Society of Great Britain while writing History of Aurangzeb in five volumes had done injustice to him. They are biased. There were many Hindu Generals in Aurangzeb's Army. In fact even Hindu or British historians do not mention anywhere that Aurangzeb removed any General or those who were occupying high post during his father Shahjahan's time on the ground of their being Hindus. Besides there are many farmars by Aurangzeb granting protections and freedom to Brahmins and Hindus to practice their religious activities freely. He also granted many villages for maintenance of the Temples in and around Bananas Chitrakoot and elsewhere. If Aurangzeb did not like the activities of Shivaji and termed it against his Kingdom and tried to keep him under his subjugation he is termed communal. But what about his action of dislodging the Muslim rulers of Adil Shahis Kingdom of Hyderabad. Similarly because he got Guru Teg Bahadur killed he is declared communal but no one talks when he got killed a Muslim Saint Shah Sarmad. Akbar opposed Rana Pratap, but he is called Secular? Aurangzeb ruled for 49/50 long years. If his policies were as anti-Hindu as is being projected entire India would have been Muslim. It is because after Aurangzeb all Moghal rulers were incompetent the Moghal Kingdom started to disintegrate. This was because of the incompetency of subsequent kings and not because of the policy of Aurangzeb. The Britishers in their long term scheme got the God gifted opportunity and started instigating all the Rajas and Nawabs to disassociate their subjugation of the weak and Ayash and incompetent Moghal Kings after Aurangzeb and instigated them to declare themselves independent of Moghal rule.

When Moghals became weak, the descendents of these very Rajputs and Iranis who were occupying high positions in Moghal Kingdom changed their loyalty to Britishers to retain their authority on High places of the Government. Common Muslim inhabitants out of Afghan migratory were already made economically weak and demoralized due to repressive policies of Moghals still they showed resistance against Britishers. But their resistance was unorganized. Due to lack of resources, they were unable to acquire better quality of arms and ammunitions which the Britishers had. Moreover Britishers had employed the Armed personnel of the Nawabs and Jageerdars. These soldiers were left high and dry by these Nawabs and Jagirdars who could not afford their salary mostly because of their *Ayashees* and protection money to the Britishers. Thus Britishers got readymade army of native people to fight against the native common men.

The British recruited soldiers for the Bengal Army from an area comprising U.P. and Western Bihar. Some 40,000 of British Bengal Army came from Oudh alone. However, the Britishers restricted the promotions of the native sepoys only upto Subedar and only in very exceptional case as Subedar Major and that was the end of promotional ladder of the Natives. Inspite of the above discriminatory treatment, the Britishers used the Bengal Army as cannon fodder in their grand design of British imperialism and expansionism and used them extensively in Burma, China, Afghan of 1839-43, Gwalior War, Sind War of 1894 and Punjab Wars and second Burma War of 1852 and then in 1852 to Crimea to fight against Russia and then Persia. Britishers used Indian troops in their sinister design of expansionism.

Back in India Britishers made Hindu Rajas believe that if they will help Muslim groups who were spearheading revolt against

Britishers, they will again become subject of Muslim rulers. This led to the Hindu Rajas and the Greedy Muslims rulers, such as Nizam of Hyderabad, Nawab of Karnatka and Mir Jaffar of Bengal Mir Sadiq of Decan (South) to side with Britishers.

As for common Hindu population was concerned they were confused and were unable to decide as to what they should do. They remained indifferent rather helped Britishers wherever they had the option to take side between Muslims and Britishers.

A.K. Biswas says:

> "Those loyal to the crown were sumptuously rewarded. Who were they? Upper caste, upper class predators and parasites. The D.M. of Gaya received a delegation on 1st August, 1857 of Gayawal Brahmins who offered to supply, in concert with the Zameendars, 3000-4000 men to fight against the freedom fighters."
>
> "Gayawal was close to Rajir where Rajwars had risen in revolt. The British could not conceal their glee. This was the elitist treason that has marked the upper classes and upper castes ever since. In post colonial India the British rule is identified with subjugation of Indian aspiration, exploitation, and tyranny. But the Gayawals had no compunction in siding with the enemy. Those Holy men of Gaya redefined the meaning of treason and thought it patriotism to sell the nation to foreigners, just like today."

The commissioner William Taylor in his book "Thirty-eight Years in India" published in London in 1981-82 in two volumes described, p. 193, Volume II, the incidence of revolt by the Prisoners of Arrah Jail in 1855:

> "I managed by a little ingenuity to sow dissent between Hindus and Mussalmans, representing that the rebellion was caused, for their own purposes, by the latter."
>
> This, he said, could be achieved with the help of his friend Babu Kunwar Singh of Jagdeeshpur.
>
> (Also p. 198, "Memoirs of William Taylor" by Chaturbhuj).

The claim of William Taylor gives the insight of his Character rather the clear mentality of Britishers as to how they used the policy of divide and rule. He knew that only Patna city had the population of over 3,00,000. He himself mentions, "a long proportion of whom were Mohammedans and a fact which was of infinite importance, it was the headquarter of the Fanatical Sect called Wahabees."

Wahabee Sect of Muslims were opposed to the Britishers apart from political reasons, they found that Britishers were destroying the basic Indian and Islamic culture and are spreading Christianity in India. They found Christians more close to Jews. Thus Wahabees were preaching among their followers against Christianity. Consequently against the emergence of British in India.

The remaining Muslim's groups including Ulema who were actually working against the establishment of British rule had realized that over the last about 100 years the East India Company which came in India to do business were infact exploiting the entire populace of India. They were infact aiming to enslave India. This naked fact was not visualized by the then Rajas, Nawabs because they were bereft of any National feelings but were blind folded by greed of their individual power. They had become just puppets of Britishers and were busy in their "Aiyashees" with no concern for the people or the country. The Hindu population, not realizing the consequences were playing in the hands of Britishers with the hope Britishers will help them in establishing their own rule.

Karl Marx also described, p. 33, the condition of the Indian society as under:

> "Indian Society has no history at all, at least no known history. What we call its History, is but the History of the successive intruders, who founded their empires on the passive basis of that un-resisting and unchanging society. The question, therefore, is not whether English had a right to conquer India, but whether we are to prefer India conquered by the Turk, by the Persian, by the Russian or be conquered by the Britain."

English has to fulfill double mission in India:

(a) *One destructive:* i.e. the annihilation of old Asiatic Society.

(b) *Other regenerating:* i.e. the laying of the material foundations of the Western Society in Asia.

"The British were the first conquerors superior, and, therefore in-accessible to Hindu civilisation. They destroyed it by breaking up the Native Committees by uprooting the native, industry, and by levelling all that was great and elevated in the native society. The historic pages of their rule in India report hardly anything beyond that destruction. The work of re-generation hardly transpires through the heap of ruins."

Situation in 18th century was:

(a) Maratha ruled Bombay, Gujarat, Rajputana and were trying to capture Delhi, Bengal and Asam but were defeated in 1761 in Panipat.

(b) French were ruling in Madras.

(c) Nizam in Hyderabad.

(d) Teepu Sultan in Mysore till 1799.

Between 1803-06, East India Company was virtually ruling Hindustan.

On the reference of book "Sultan Jamhoor" Hazrat Teepu Sultan Shaheed, pp. 65-66, 194-95, "Tehreek-e-Azadi Men Ulema Ka Kirdar" quoted Colonel Wilk after the Shahadat of Teepu:

"After the defeat of Teepu Sultan in 1799 it was found that in every and each Indian States, however, small or big, Teepu's appeal to remove the Britishers and other foreigners, all should unite."

Unfortunately, no one responded. Rather Nizam, Marathas and others sided with Britishers to fight with Teepu. Teepu after occupying the control of Mysore declared his first and foremost responsibility to:

"It is my duty that till I am alive, I should engage myself to the Jehad to liberate and protect the honour of my country from the presence of Britishers. Thousands of people may have to lay their lives for the sake of the Nation, but the Nation is Supreme."

He further declared:

"O! my Motherland Hindustan, my love is for you, my life and my existence is only for you, my blood and my life is only for you."

(Ref. "Shere Mysore" by Quaiser Mustafa, p. 4 from book "Shere Hindustan" by Khursheed Mustafa Rizvi, pp. 46, 191, "Tehreek-e-Azadi Men Ulema Ka Kirdar".)

After getting no response of unity from India rulers Teepu turned to, Afghanistan, Iran, Turkey and other Arab and Muslim countries seeking their help to remove foreigners from Indian soil. Sultan Saleem the Sali-se-Khaleefa of Turkee instead helping Teepu offered to mediate between Teepu and Britishers. Teepu wrote letters to all the Muslim world rulers. In one of his letters, to the ruler of Afghanistan Zaman Shah, Teepu suggested that some competent Moghal Dynasty person be placed on Delhi throne in place of the incompetent Shah Alam. (Ref.: "Shere Hindustan", p. 147 and Secret correspondence of Teepu Sultan, pp. 148-52, 202-03, "Tehreek-e-Azadi Men Ulema Ka Kirdar").

When Teepu found Welzalee along with Nizam and Marathas, preparing to attack Teepu he sent urgent messages to the rulers of Afghanistan and Iran to help. The ruler of Afghanistan Zaman Shah immediately rushed in person alongwith strong force of 33 thousand army personnel and reached upto Lahore. However, Welzalee came to know the Teepu's approach to Afghanistan and Iran. He immediately deputed one Saiyed Mehdi Ali Khan a Shia from Moradabad and paid him Rs. 2,80,000/ to rush to Iran and persuade Shah Iran Fateh Ali Shah Qachar, to attack on Afghanistan, so that Zaman Shah is forced to go back and is not able to help Teepu. The Ghaddre Watan and Zameer Frosh, Saiyed Mehdi Ali Khan did exactly the same and made the Shah Iran believe him that Zaman Shah is killing thousands of Shias daily in Afghanistan. Shah Iran, Fateh Ali Shah Qachar foolishly without verification of truth rushed and attacked on Afghanistan. Zaman Shah after hearing the attack on his own country rushed back to Afghanistan. Thus Welzalee succeeded in his scheme and attacked Mysore and was able to encircle Teepu Sultan with the help of Teepu's own Wazeers, such as Meer Qasim Ali and Mir Sadiq and few others all Shias and some Hindu officers. Teepu obtained Shahadat and his declaration:

> "India is for Indian" ("Tareekhe Sultanat-e-Khudabad", p. 14) remained unfulfilled and India became the colony of Britishers.

10

The Jehad-e-Azaadi by Saiyed Ahmad Shaheed and Wahabee Movement as Described by Various Historians and the Role of Muslims

That the movement of 1857 and even few years later was purely a movement of Muslims of the country be it Wahabees Sect or others but only by Muslims and the total concentration of the Britisher was against Muslims only and no other.

The book, "Tehreek-e-Azaadi Men Ulema Ka Kirdar" before 1857, p. 396, describes the condition in Bihar as under:

At the end of 1845 AD, the Government of East India Company, became aware of the conspiracy that Danapur's Native army was being instigated by certain elements against the British. Britishers gave due importance to this information. The book quotes, G.B. Malleson, William Taylor, William Hunter as under:

G.B. Malleson:

"In 1845 a group of conspirators were busy to generate revolt in Patna. They were distributing cash to the native armed men. One document was captured, which contained the names of about 100 prominent families. It also contained the names of certain important people of Patna such as Welayat Ali and Enayat Ali the deputies of Saiyed Ahmed Shaheed."

(*Source:* Hindustan's Wahabee Tehreek, p. 208.)

This Welayat Ali is different from the Saiyed Welayat Ali Khan the grandson of Mir Abdullah.

William Taylor:

> "For the last many years Patna was being considered as the Centre of conspiracy and angry people. In 1846 one very dangerous conspiracy was discussed, in which many Muslims of Patna and its surroundings were found involved. In the conspiracy efforts were made to instigate the native soldiers to revolt. The 1846 conspiracy was considered a very big conspiracy by all knowledgeable persons of this country. The object of conspiracy was to destroy the British and to remove the British Government and re-establish the rule of Muslims."

William Hunter on happenings of 1852:

> "During same period of Patna Magistrate reported that number of Revolutionaries/ Mutineers and such organizations are increasing in the city (Patna) and the revolutionaries of the capital of British capital are openly preaching revolt. Even police was also supporting these crazy people, and out of these one had collected at his house 700 people for this very purpose so that they should be able to fight if Government takes any steps against it."

At pp. 336, 345-46 of the book, "Tehreek-e-Azadi Men Ulema Ka Kirdar," William Hunter has been further quoted:

> "The Jehad by Saiyed Saheb was against Britishers." "People in Azamgarh specially 'Ansarees' revolted against Britishers on the call of Saiyed Saheb. E.N. Kamarao has referred a report of a British Officer in which it is mentioned that being influenced from Saiyed Saheb's call of Jehad many people more particularly 'Noor Bafaon' (the weavers) of Azamgarh revolted."
>
> (Ref. "Hazrat Saiyed Ahmed Shaheed Aur Unke Tehreeke-Islah Wa Jehad", p. 28).

> "Saiyed Ahmad Shaheed wanted complete revolution in the entire country against the Britishers. Wherever, he himself could not reach he deputed his confident deputies (Khulfa). In those deputies (*Khulfa*) Maulana Welayat Ali Azeemabadi, Maulana Karamatali Jaunpuri, Maulana Saiyed Mohammed Ali Rampuri are prominent. He deputed Maulana Welayat Ali Azeemabadi to Hydrabad Daken, Maulana Karamatali Jaunpuri to Bengal and Maulana Mohammed Ali Rampuri to Madras."

Saiyed Amir who was leading the mutiny in Peshwar. The Britishers called him in contempt a mendicant (person living on begging). See T.R.E. Holm's "A History of Indian Mutiny, p. 364). Similarly William Taylor described Maulvi Ahmedullah Madrasi, p. 233 of Chaturbhuj's book as "Notorious Wahabee Traitor." What a pity the person fighting for the nation is called "Traitor"?

Similar was the object of Maulana Saiyed Ahmed Shaheed who was engaged in Sarhad (Peshawar) against Sikhs and British.

The British are so much scared of Saiyed Ahmed Shaheed that even after passage of over 150 years the British historian, Charles Allen's new book, "God's Terrorist" suggests that Wahabism, the creed that Al-Qaeda believes in, existed in India in the 18th century and that Saiyed Ahmed was India's Osama."

Charles Allen further writes, that the thesis, as the introduction suggest, is that the modern day "Jehad" has its roots in the late 18th century in Saudi Arabia, when an intolerant strand of Islam is adopted by a preacher. Al-Wahab. (Muhammed Ibne Abdul Wahab who advocated purging Islam of Modern accretions and relying strictly on the Quran and Hadith.)

Hindustan Times, Daily, New Delhi dated 19.11.2006 in an article by Shevlin Sebstani quotes from the said book "God's Terrorist":

> "He takes it from teaching of Ibn Taymiyya, a 14th century jurist of Damascus. This is later called Wahabism, which is deeply belligerent and hostile towards Shias, Sunnis, Christians, Jews and Hindus. Their argument is very simple:

you either believe in our version of Islam or you die." It is this creed that is the religious base of Al-Qaida and other Jehadi outfit. But the storming revelation is that Wahabism was present in India since the late 18th Century. A young man, Saiyed Ahmad, who was the Osama Bin Laden of his days goes to Mecca for Haj and returns with this new ideology and starts preaching it all over the country. In Mumbai, the Sunnis unit to condemn him. Most Muslims in India rejected the ideology. Ahmad first Jehad wȧs against Sikhs but he was killed in the famous massacar of Balakot on May 8, 1831."

The following description of Saiyed Ahmad Shaheed will show how wrong is Charles Allen.

Maulana Husain Ahmed Deobandi described, p. 435, Book "Baghi-e-Hindustan" (See also "Tehreek Azadi Men Ulema Ka Kirdar" from pp. 311-58).

"On the call of Jehad by Saiyed Saheb, the people of Azamgarh specially 'Ansarees' revolted against Britishers. E.N. Kamarao has referred a report of a British officer in which it is mentioned that being influenced from Saiyed Saheb's Call of Jehad many people more particularly (Noor Bafon) of Azamgarh revolted."

"The very object of Saiyed Saheb's movement was to finish the British occupation and power from Indian Soil because both Hindus and Muslims were the sufferers. Because of this reason Saiyed Saheb invited Hindus also to join in his strife to remove Britishers from Indian Soil. He told both Hindus and Muslims that, they will join him with clear and only object to free India from the foreign rule. Thereafter, who will rule the country (Hindu or Muslim) you should not bother. Whosoever (Hindus or Muslims) will be capable to rule, will rule. May be both."

(Professor: Khaleeq Ahmed Nizam's "Hazrat Saiyed Ahmed Shaheed Aur Unke Tehreek-e-Islah Wa Jehad", p. 28).

Even William Dalrymple in his book "Last Moghal", pp. 83-84 writes about Saiyed Ahmad Shaheed:

> "He wrote to the rulers of central Asia asking them to join hands in liberating India from British rule."
>
> "A Wahabee conspiracy in Delhi itself, seizing the correspondence of the Fanatic Maulvies preaching a crusade against British." (In both the above observations the reference is British and not Hindus.)

Saiyed Ahmad Shaheed fought against Sikhs because they were unleashing cruelty over Muslims and were supporters of British design to enslave India.

He never preached to fight or kill Hindus as malafidely suggest Charles Allen or Shevlin Sebstani.

One will find that Peer Ali Khan had, in his group Hindus, Muslims, Wahabees and non-Wahabees, all together. He opted a flag with Blue and White colour neither saffron nor green. This was the flag which Teepu Sultan used. This shows that Peer Ali Khan and Teepu Sultan both were true Nationalist and secular.

Further, T.R.E. Homes' "A History of India Mutiny", pp. 179-82, records the condition in Patna division:

> "Most of the Zameendars indeed were believed to be well disposed; but the Magistrates generally expressed a conviction that the Mohammedan portion of the population was thoroughly disaffected (Not satisfied with the situation therefore lacking loyalty) and that, if any disturbance occurred at Patna, the infection would probably spread throughout the province."
>
> "The burden to maintain law and order for the benefit of British in Bengal and Bihar was on the shoulders of Frederick Halliday the Lt. Governor of Bengal and his representative, William Taylor the Commissioner of Patna."
>
> "Patna with its hundred and fifty thousand inhabitants was a hot bed of Mohammedans, intrigue; (to make secret

plans to harm) and the memory of a great conspiracy which had been discovered some ten years before, remained to warn the English that they were surrounded by a population among whom there were many restless spirits, secretly longing to over throw their (English) power, and re-establish 'A Mohammedan dynasty.' (This is what Britishers were telling the Hindu population not to support Muslims). When the first symptoms of revolt appeared, there was hardly a man in Bihar who did not look to Patna as the head center of disloyalty." *Source:* Patna Crisis by Taylor, pp. 21-22, 24.)

G.W. Forrest, p. 402, notes:

"On the 21st of May Herbert Edward discovered at Peshawar that the most rancorous and seditious letters had been intercepted from Mohammedan bigots in Patna and Thanesar to soldiers of the 64th Native infantry, reveling in the atrocities that had been committed in Hindustan on the men, women, and children of the 'Nazarenes' and sending them messages from their own mothers that they should emulate these deeds and if they fell in the attempt they would at least go to heaven, and their deaths in such a case would be pleasant news at home."

My salute to the mothers of the sons of the country, who were mostly Muslims, who told their sons to fight for the country even if they are killed they will attain the Martyrdom.

At pp. 402-03, G.W. Forrest says:

"The Bengal Government refused to believe in the Wahabee conspiracy. It was after Wahabees of Patna had plunged us into several frontier expeditions that the machinations of their wide spread conspiracy were laid bare. Eight years after the Mutiny of 1857, in 1865, eleven Wahabees, five of them being residents of Patna were tried for attempting to wage war and abetting."

The chief conspirator was the High priest of Patna (Haji Ahmedullah). He was found guilty and sentenced to transportation for life.

"The brother of the High Priest was one of the Wahabees arrested by Taylor. He was after the Mutiny, appointed by the Bengal Government to a responsible office on a handsome salary, and made member of the Patna committee of public instruction. In 1865, he was tried for a similar offence, found guilty, and awarded transportation for life."

"The Story of Wahabee conspiracy is full of instruction to the English statesman and Indian administrator. The atmosphere may be calm on the surface under British rule, but beneath a thin crust the volcanic fires of fanaticism and bigotry still smoulder, wide-spreading religious movements of which the authorities are unconscious arise, and there are always men like the highly educated Wahabee conspirator, who will use them with oriental craft and secrecy to subvert an alien Government, however, benevolent be its intention."

The above observations by Britishers trying to show Muslims and Wahabees as conspirator, fanatic etc., was because they faught with them for the protection of the liberty of the country if gets support from Indians, is not it a matter of shame for such Indians?

11

The Capture of Secret Letter from Danapore Cantonment Taylor's Action to Arrest the Wahabee Leaders. The Silence of Kunwar Singh and His Friendly Relations with Taylor Who Wanted to Help Kunwar Singh Financially

On the evening of 7th June, 1857 while William Taylor the Commissioner of Patna Division was driving through the race course, he was informed that some conspiracy is being hatched and the regiments at Danapur is likely to revolt and rise against British rule.

Sameday two envelops containing secret communications by the activist from Danapur Cantonment were by mistake delivered to a wrong sepoy in Patna. The Sepoy innocently handed it to his local commanding officer. The Commanding officer who was also Indian but loyal to British immediately handed it to Taylor.

The letters were meant to be delivered to Hazara Singh who in turn was to deliver to Peer Ali Khan. The message in substance was that the soldiers of Danapur will revolt and then will march to Patna (Azeemabad) and will seize the Treasury there and will join the local people's movement.

The messenger after realizing the mistake rushed back to Danapur and informed the mistake. The organizers of Danapur decided to delay the revolt. Taylor had become active after reading the message and had blocked all communication from Danapur to Patna.

Taylor after getting the information immediately sought the additional Sikh force which he received under the command of Rettrey.

On arrival at Azeemabad Rettrey informed to Taylor that his Sikh regiment throughout the way were taunted and insulted by the local people because the Sikh soldiers were loyal to British and were infact suppressing the movement by other Indians.

On 8th June, 1857 Taylor sent full report to Mr. Halliday the Lt. Governor, of the impending dangers in Azeemabad. However, Halliday did not agree that Patna was in any danger. But Taylor was convinced that danger was hovering over Patna. He saw that only possibility to check it was in resolutely repressing the Mohammedans of Patna and in preventing all communication between them and the Danapur Sepoys. (Ref. Patna Crisis, pp. 35, 37 42, 44).

Taylor was convinced and agreed with the opinion of the Magistrates and assessed the situation and was satisfied that as for as Hindu Zameendars are concerned they were not going to support the revolt because their interest was best protected with British rule and with the help of British these Zameendars were infact exploiting and were looting the poor peasants. However, Taylor thought that the report is indicating towards Wahabees only, hence immediate action was necessary to contain Wahabees. He did not realize that the Danapur upheaval was not linked with Wahabees, but another group was active behind the same. He was worried about the Mohammedans who could not be trusted if any revolt takes place, they will immediately join the revolutionist. (A History of Indian Mutiny, pp. 181-82 by T.R.E. Homes).

In a narrative report of Marshman in the said book and in Saturday review dated September 9, 1857, it is written:

> "Most of the Hindus appeared to be either indifferent or apprehensive, but where ever a Mohammedan was seen there was a scowl (*angry look*) on his brow."
>
> (A History of Indian Mutiny by T.R.E. Holms, pp. 260-89).

Taylor was worried and wanted to check the revolt before it takes place. The British population around Azeemabad (Patna) were very much scared. Some of them even left their postings. Taylor persuaded them to stay and assured them that he will take full care and protect them.

Taylor was of the firm opinion that Patna (Azeemabad) is in danger and that Danapur soldiers are at the verge of Mutiny. Taylor was of the opinion that unless he disarmed the Danapur soldiers he will not be able to save British control over Patna. Accordingly Taylor against the orders of the Lt. Governor of Bengal Mr. Halliday insisted with the General Lloyd Commanding Officer of Danapur to disarm all native soldiers except the Sikhs who were loyal to Britishers. However, General Lloyd also did not agree and tried to convince Taylor that he trusts his native soldiers and will hold them and that there was no need to disarm them. Taylor was not satisfied and considered to adopt other method to satisfy his ego.

Taylor then thought that only way he nip in the bud the danger of revolt was to use repressive attitude against Mohammedans of Patna and surroundings and cutting all links and communication between the Mohammedans and the soldiers of Danapur, because he had in his possession the two letters from Danapur Cantonment from where he came to know that there was some conspiracy going on between the Danapur non-Sikh Sepoys and the some group of Muslims in Patna.

Taylor silently pondered over the situation. He found that the richer sections of Muslim community do not appear to pose any danger. In fact, one of the grandsons of Mir Abdullah, Saiyed, Welayat Ali Khan was almost a daily "Musaheb" of Taylor and provided valuable information of the city to Taylor. He further thought that common populace of Muslims being very poor were not in a position to commit any armed revolt as no one was there to provide them funds for the same and all the Arms were already confiscated by Taylor. Still he found that out of Muslims the most dangerous inhabitants of Bihar were Wahabee Muslims. They had close organization widely extended throughout India and their followers totally submitted and strictly followed their Maulvis like, ROMAN Catholic to Pope.

Hence, Taylor decided to first rein the Wahabees. It was not possible to arrest all the Wahabees or to have check on all of them. He knew that the followers of Wahabee Sect will blindly follow their leader as Roman Catholics follow the Pope. Taylor immediately hatched a plan to arrest the three prominent leaders of Wahabees Sect of Azeemabad. They were Shah Ahmad Hussain, Maulvi Waezul Haque and prominent of them Haji Ahmadullah all three of Azeemabad.

Accordingly, on 18th June, 1857, Taylor sent invitation letters to most of the respectable native citizens of Patna for a meeting at his house. The meeting was scheduled to be held on 25th June, 1857, at Taylors residence. (In some books the date is mentioned, 19th June, 1857 and at others 25th June, 1857.)

The invitees among others included Shah Ahmed Hussain, Maulvi Waezul Haque, Haji Ahmadullah, Babu Kunwar Singh of Jagdishpur, Distt. Shahbad. All the invitees were assembled on 19th/ 25th June at the residence of William Taylor. Babu Kunwar Singh did not come and wrote back that due to illness he was not in a position to undertake the journey. Taylor told the assembled people that some people just for the sake of mischief are spreading the news that the bullets contained cow and Pig fat (*charbee*). It is being rumored that Britishers want to convert Indians as Christian. He offered that they can examine it, there is no fat of any kind. Taylor told the assembled people that they do not intend to convert anyone to Christianity. He said that Padris convert to Christianity only those who are discarded by Indian society as untouchable (*Achoot*) or those who are not happy of their social status and wants to join Christianity. British never used force or raised sword to convert people to Christianity said Taylor.

The Commissioner sought the co-operation of the people to maintain calm and persuade the people not to do any thing which may be considered against the British Administration. Every one present there expressed agreement with the Commissioner.

Thereafter Taylor declared that the meeting is dispersed. Those assembled started leaving, relieved as if (*Jaan Bachee Lakhon Paye*) however, the moment the three Wahabee leaders Shah

Ahmed Husain, Maulvi Waezul Haque and Haji Ahmadullah, were about to leave Taylor asked Haji Ahmadullah that you three people will wait as I have to discuss something with you three. When everyone had left Taylor took all the three in his personal office and told Haji Ahmadullah that he is aware that their followers are instigating the people to undertake "Jehad" against British rule. Haji Ahmadullah replied that their group (sect) only Preach Islam and do not indulge in political activities. Taylor said that he has information that Wahabees were involved in the revolt at Afghan borders and he has further information that till Wahabees are free they will continue to misguide people to undertake "Jehad" against the British rule. Finding his followers being single-out Haji Ahmadullah got furious but kept his anger under control and said that, as if our people (followers) are "Ah-le-Hades" and not Wahabee? What did Haji Ahmadullah meant with this remark I am unable to understand? Because the Wahabees are the followers of Muhammed Ibne Abdul Wahab of Saudi Arabia who advocated purging Islam of Modern accretions and relying strictly on the Quran and Hadith. Ahle Hadith also believes in the same. However, Taylor ignoring the comment of Haji Abdullah told him that it is his final decision that until complete normalcy is attained you three will remain under his custody, and they will be kept in a Bungalow with all the facilities of a decent living according to their status.

Thereafter Commissioner called Major Rettrey and asked him to take the three under his custody. While leaving the Commissioner paused and told Haji Ahmadullah that, "you are under my custody but your father and other family members are still free. Now it is upto, you three to see that your followers are under control failing which I will not stand guarantee to your safety and also that of your family." In this treacherous way Taylor arrested the Wahabee leaders and ensured the behaviour of Wahabees through their leaders.

However, the news of arrest of the these Wahabee leaders angered most of the Muslim population of Azeemabad irrespective of their faith or Sect, because Haji Ahmadullah was respected by all the Sect of Muslims.

The Wahabee's wanted Britishers to go, but they had no support from General masses except those who blindly believed in the philosophy of Wahabeeism. The Wahabees of Sadiqpur were rich. They had their followers throughout India. But due to the reason of their being follower of a particular Sect, the Muslim community in general, did not have any truck with them. Secondly majority of Hindus were not interested in revolt as they thought that if British will go Muslim rule will come back hence they did not support any group led by Muslims. Inspite of this Peer Ali Khan who was not the follower of Wahabeeism, still to attain the real object of independence and to make the revolt against British, successful, tried to have some understanding with the Wahabees of Azeemabad. Besides his main dependence was on the Sepoys of Danapur. Peer Ali Khan had organized the revolt in the non-Sikh Sepoys in Danapur and Waris Ali Khan, who claimed to be from the Royal Family of Delhi was working on the rank of Jamadar in Trihut Police, was one of the main links between Peer Ali Khan and the Sepoys of Danapur.

But the prematured arrest of Waris Ali on 23.06.1857 in Muzaffarpur and upon his person found bundle of letters implicating in the rebellious movement by Ali Kareem, and the wrong delivery of the two envelops containing the programme of Revolt by the regiment of Danapur gave a big set back to the programme of Peer Ali Khan. The arrest of Waris Ali was kept secret by Taylor for interrogation purposes and to find out the names of his followers.

It appears the British authorities could not get any detail of the impending revolt from the two letters because they were coded One referred to a major enterprise from East to West in which extensive profit was to be made. Other spoke of a savory "Pulao" ready for eating and urged its recipient to bring all his friends to enjoy it, even if it meant making sacrifices. ("God's Terrorist", p. 144)

However, the information of Waris Ali's arrest was conveyed to Peer Ali by Sardar Hazara Singh who used to provide information to Peer Ali Khan. Hazara Singh was a Sepoy and a friend of Waris Ali. Treating Peer Ali as friend of Waris Ali used to divulge certain information to Peer Ali Khan. Hazara Singh though a Sikh and one of the army men in the Sikh regiment under the command of Major Rettrey, was close to Waris Ali because both were from Delhi. Hazara Singh was on duty to guard the opium godown in Patna where Dr. Lloyel was the Assistant to the Agent of the Opium Godown.

After Waris Ali's arrest on 23rd June, 1857 he was brought to Patna for interrogation but the information was kept a close secret and was interrogated by William Taylor personally. (pp. 408-09, G.W. Forrest book). Thereafter, an associate of Waris Ali a Muslim Sepoy took the place of Waris Ali and started instigating the Danapur Sikh Sepoys to revolt against British. Sikhs being loyal to British, immediately reported this to their Commanding Officer Major Rettrey. Major Rettrey arrested him and brought him to Patna where on the orders of Taylor he was hanged on 25.06.1857 even before Waris Ali was hanged. Here it is important to note that from 23.06.1857 till 4th July, 1857, Peer Ali Khan was not arrested. It shows that Waris Ali inspite of Torture as well as lurement by Taylor did not disclose the name of Peer Ali Khan.

Shad Azeemabadi in his book "Peer Ali" at p. 15, rightly says that Peer Ali Khan was a poor man and had undertaken the task of liberating India from British when the country was not ready and prepared for the same. People were illiterate, and the society was full of all sorts of social and political ills. Peer Ali knew, he was too small a fry to challenge the Britishers and knew that he may not succeed but he was determined to lit the light of freedom movement for future generation to follow and was willing to give the extreme sacrifice, which he did.

Peer Ali Khan's group could have got some help from some old Zameendars whose holdings either was confiscated by the Britishers or was about to be confiscated. Out of them the Zameendar of Dumri, Ali Kareem who was fully in support of Peer Ali Khan, but after the arrest of Waris Ali, Ali Kareem was exposed and Taylor had put all his attention to arrest him, which made Ali Kareem on the run and kept on moving from place to place to avoid arrest and execution, hence became irrelevant as for as the movement of Peer Ali Khan was concerned.

Thomas Rettrey in his accounts of events writes:

"A notorious rebel, Ali Kareem who resided at a village Doomrie was permitted to escape. His house was searched. Taylor discovered from the papers found in Ali Kareem's house that the Daroghah of Mozuffarpore named Waris Ali was one of the principal conspirators. Taylor silently deputed the Magistrate to seize him and send him to Patna. Taking four friends, planters in the neighbourhood, with him, in the middle of the night reached to the thana, found the Daroghah (Waris Ali) booted and spurred sitting on a carpet writing letters, his horse outside ready saddled and a pony loaded with his persona goods. On the person the Daroghah was found a letter from Ali Kareem requesting him to come with all haste. Number of letters were found in the possession of Waris Ali together with a lot of gold mohars, shawls and silver dishes not usual in the possession of a Daroghah on Rs.10 or Rs. 12 rupees a month. There is little doubt but that this man merely took the office of Daroghah to act as a shy to the rebels. Waris Ali was a good looking of immense size and unfortunately when first string up the rope broke and he fell to the ground. He then looked upon the crowd of lookers on and asked, was there no true Mohammedan present who could come to his rescue? No one moved. There were only few Sikhs presents as guard." No one came to his rescue.

Second one was Zameendar of Jagishpur Babu Kunwar Singh who was friend of Taylor. Taylor himself stated and believed, "he was driven into rebellion by the short sightedness of Bengal Government."

The help which Peer Ali Khan expected from Danapur Sepoys was not now available as by that time the Soldiers at Danapur were not ready to revolt as their programme was got exposed due to the arrest of Waris Ali and the delivery of two messages to a wrong Sepoy at Patna which fell in the hands of Taylor. But Peer Ali could not have withheld his revolt as he himself was exposed due to the arrest of Waris Ali Khan and the speed with which

Taylor was moving ahead to curb the revolt. Peer Ali Khan was left with the only expectation of support from the angry people of Patna who were angry because of the arrest of Haji Ahmedullah and others on 19/25.06.1857, who inspite of being Wahabee was respected by majority of Muslims irrespective of their affinity of Sect. This helped Peer Ali Khan in his movement and thus Peer Ali Khan was able to muster support of hundreds of people on 3rd July, 1857 in his agitation and revolt against British rule.

While Taylor put his full attention in the pursuit to arrest Ali Kareem, ignoring Peer Ali Khan not worth his personal attention at the said moment. This gave Peer Ali Khan breather, hence he rushed through his plan to attack before Taylor pounced on him and his followers. Peer Ali Khan after the arrest of Waris Ali wanted Danapur regiment to advance their revolt to 3rd July, 1857 in the morning and start moving towards Patna, so that Taylor gets busy at Danapur and in the meantime Peer Ali Khan along with his follower, including some willing Wahabees will revolt in the afternoon of 3rd July, 1857 at Patna. Danapur soldiers were expected to reach Patna by the afternoon and join Peer Ali's group. Peer Ali Khan had made a flag for his group which was white and blue, 3 ft. long and 2 ft. wide. This was similar flag which Teepu Sultan had hoisted on Sri Ranga Patan and fought against Britishers under the said flag. Peer Ali Khan declared to his followers that this will be the flag of independent India. Peer Ali Khan was not fighting for restoration of Muslims rule but for avoiding the slavery of India by Britishers. His fight, was for an Independent and secular India and not for a Muslim or Hindu India.

12

The Peer Ali Khan had to Prepone His Programme as the Actions of His Associates and His Involvement was Got Exposed due to the Premature Arrest of Waris Ali and Capture of Two Secret Letters

Peer Ali Khan was using his shop in Patna as his base of the Movement. Shad Azeemabadi described, that, on 2nd July, 1857 in the evening one of the follower Immamuddin was sitting with Peer Ali Khan in the shop, who asked Peer Ali Khan as to how he planed to fight and survive with few of his followers and few old junked Guns Peer Ali Khan could arrange for his followers and till the army from Danapur reaches to Patna. (The guns which Peer Ali Khan could arrange was probably with the help of one Maulvi Medhi a patrolling Magistrate of Patna city who was arrested by Taylor on 20.06.1857 and sentenced to death without trial.) Peer Ali Khan replied, "if eight people rise it will create 800 followings which will bring upto 8000 and so on. What is needed the determination." He further said, "Azaadi Ke Deewane top ke gole se nahin darte." Peer Ali Khan was further depending on the people of the Northern Bihar where Britishers were getting cultivated "Indigo Plants (Neel)" and were treating the local people worst than dogs. Indulged in rape, violent beating of the poor was a common phenomenon. Peer Ali Khan expected that these people will revolt, the moment they will find any group fighting Britishers. Peer Ali knew that Danapur soldiers were not sure to revolt by 3rd July, 1857 because of the capture of the two letters but he had to keep the moral of his group high for the revolt on 3rd July, 1857.

Peer Ali Khan knew that time was running out of his hand. He was aware that Taylor will be able to catch him any day or moment. He further knew that he was left with only three options. Either he also runs away like Ali Kareem or silently surrenders as a coward or jumps in the fray and attain the martyrdom. He chose the 3rd option. Accordingly, on 3rd July, 1857 with few people at his command and without waiting for the army of Danapur to come to his help, he declared the war of Independence. He knew that he has very little rather no chance to succeed still he chose to fight. He started his action with the hope that people will join or at least with the movement, he may succeed to arouse the passion of the people, against the British rule.

Taylor did not know anything about Peer Ali Khan, as to who he was. Taylor knew only his name when his name alongwith Ali Kareem was found mentioned in the letters captured from Waris Ali. Taylor had asked Maula Baksh the Dy. Commissioner to find out all about Peer Ali Khan. He asked Maula Baksh to concentrate on the immediate arrest of Ali Kareem because Ali Kareem was a rich Zameendar and had the resources to mobalise support. He considered Peer Ali Khan merely an insignificant helper of Ali Kareem and a small try to deal with at later stage. It was only in the night of 1st July, 1857, Welayat Ali the rich Nawab acting as the informer of Britishers told the Taylor that there is a person with the name of Peer Ali who sells books, near the Haweli of Padri in a small shop and probably has came from Lucknow, but when, not known. The commissioner, instructed Dewan Maula Baksh to keep Peer Ali Khan into his vigil and find out full details about him. Peer Ali Khan got the news of Taylor's instructions, hence on 2nd July, 1857, Peer Ali Khan decided to advance the agitation and decided to declare war of Independence on 3rd July, 1857, irrespective of any help coming from Danapur or not. As he knew that Danapore Sepoys will not be able to come to his support at least for 2/3 weeks now hence he decided to revolt on 3rd July, 1857, itself and had a closed door meeting with his very close friends in his shop in the night of 2nd July, 1857.

According to Shad Azeemabadi on 3rd July, 1857, after Namaz Zohar, Peer Ali's friends specially, Immamuddin, Budhan Jan,

Ghaseeta Khaleefa, Ghaseeta Khan, Ausaf Husain, Nandu Kahar, Shekh Gulam Abbas assembled at the shop of Peer Ali followed by about 200 more people. The entire process was so sudden that authorities could not realize the real intention of the people assembled there, after the Zohar Namaz. The Guns about 50 procured by Peer Ali Khan were distributed. Ghulam Abbas was made the flag bearer and was handed over the Blue and White flag. After this Peer Ali Khan closed his shop. Peer Ali Khan then instructed Nandu Kahar to stand at the Haweli of Padri and keep watch and ensure that no one leaves the Haweli to reach Gulzar Bagh, the headquarter of British establishments. Peer Ali Khan further advised his people that no one will even touch injure or kill the women and children of the Britishers. Thereafter, Peer Ali Khan alongwith Shekh Gulam Abbas the flag bearer marched with slogan against British and their rule. After seeing the slogan shouting people led by Peer Ali Khan the Padri got scared and ran towards the Gulzar Bagh where the headquarters of Taylor and other officials were situated. In the way he stopped near the opium (*Afyoon*) Godown and explained the position to Dr. Lloyel and went ahead.

Mr. Chaturbhuj in his book, titled "Memoirs of William Taylor, p. 286 has extracted from Sir J. Kaye's book "Sepoy War" Vol-III and p. 296, reproduced as under:

> "But on the evening of the 3rd July, 1857, the long threatened Patna rising occurred.......... At the period on the 3rd of July already indicated some 200 Mohammedan fanatics, led by one Peer Ali Khan, a book seller, noted for his enthusiasm for his religion and his hatred of the English, summoning by beat of drum others to join them rushed, calling upon Allah, towards the Roman catholic Church, situated in the very heart of the city."..............
>
> "Meanwhile and before the Sikhs had reached the spot Dr. Lloyel, the assistant to the opium agent, hearing the uproar and thinking that his presence might overawe the rioters, had galloped to the scene of action. As he

approached the crowd several shots were fired at him. By one of those he was killed."

Here Sir J. Kaye did not thought better to mention that Dr. Lloyel was not alone, he was accompanied with some native armed Najeebs as well as few armed Sikh Sepoys. He himself was having his revolver as well as whip. He as a Britisher was also full of arrogance and looked upon Indians nothing more than insects from dirty Gutter and tried to over run the crowd as if they were not human being and fired shots from his revolver on the crowd and simultaneously used his whip also, the Najeebs as well as Sikh Sepoy also attacked the crowd and provoked the agitators to counter attack in which Dr. Lloyal was got killed.

"The sight of a fallen European stimulated the fanaticism of the crowd, and produced on them the effect which the taste of blood arouses in a hungry tiger. They pushed onwards with renewed enthusiasm, their numbers being augmented at every step. In a very few minutes, however, they found themselves face to face with Rettray's 150 Sikhs. Between the opposing parties, far from sympathy, there was hatred of race, the hatred of religion, on the one side the newly aroused fanaticism on the other the longed for opportunity to repay many a covert insult. It can well be imagined what followed. There was not a moment of parlay. The rival parties instantaneously chased. The next day and the day following, the city was searched for the king leaders of the out break. Thirty-one were apprehended (they do not mention the number of those killed). Amongst them were Peer Ali Khan, the actual leader, and Shekh Ghaseeta, the confidential servant of Lootf Ali Khan, the richest banker in the City...............
"Fourteen were tried and executed without delay. With them likewise was hanged the Waris Ali......... Two–the two above named (Peer Ali Khan and Lootf Ali)–were remanded for further examination."......

"It was clearly proved that Peer Ali Khan was a main agent for promoting a crusade against English that for months he and the Shekh Ghaseeta above mentioned had engaged and kept in pay numerous men who should be ready, when called upon, to fight. But these operations had required a large outlay. Peer Ali Khan was poor. His associate Ghaseeta, was hand of great banker. But though it might have been fairly presumed that the great banker was implicated, no proceedings were, for the moment taken against him.

The two men, Peer Ali Khan and Ghaseeta, were tried and hanged Lootf Ali, arraigned subsequently on the charge of harbouring a mutinous sepoy, and acquitted by the Judge on the ground of insufficient evidence, was promptly released, and shortly afterwards was welcomed and honoured as a martyr by the successor of Mr. Taylor. But the outbreak was suppressed. It has been premature. As Peer Ali admitted Mr. Taylor's strong measures had forced his hand, and compelled him to strike before he was ready. But for those strong measures the conspiracy *would have been silently hatched until the outbreak at Danapur should have given it the signal for explosion."*

(Pp. 297-98, Memoirs of William Taylor)

The above narration also proves the intelligence of Peer Ali Khan, his commitment to the National cause and loyalty to Lootf Ali Khan, in not mentioning his name except that he was forced to prepone his action due to the exposure of the plot on account of the Waris Ali Khan's arrest and capture of the two letters from Danapur Cantonment.

When the news of the agitation reached to Commissioner Taylor he ordered Major Rettery to rush a Sikh Dasta. However, before the Sikh Dasta could reach Dr. Lloyel reached near the agitator. Dr. Lloyel not realizing the mood of the people, tried to run over the crowed by the horse as if they were not human beings. Many people got injured and killed in the process. Immamuddin thundered upon Dr. Lloyel to stop his horse but Dr. Lloyel instead lashed the whip on Immamuddin and injured him. Dr. Lloyel tried to repeat the lashing of the whip on Immamuddin. Immamuddin caught hold of the whip and pulled it with force which came out from Dr. Lloyed's hand. On this in his rage Dr. Lloyel took out his pistol and abused Immamuddin and simultaneously fired on Immamuddin. The bullet hit Immamuddin in his arm and passed to the chest of one Raja out of the crowed who died instantly. Immamuddin thereafter pulled out his pistol and shot twice at Dr. Lloyel who fell down from the horse and died on the spot.

A.K. Biswas quotes from the correspondence of the Commissioner it is revealed that, he ordered the District Magistrate and S.P. Patna to proceed to the spot at once with 100 Sikhs and further ordered Major General Lloyel to send 50 Europeans to crush the rebellion.

On the arrival of Sikh soldiers they started indiscriminate and blind shooting on the crowed. Immamuddin was again injured and fell down. Peer Ali Khan tried to take him on his back but the insistent shooting by Sikh and European Police did not allow him to do so. Great number of people were killed by Sikh and European Army. Those injured were either killed or hanged without trial by Taylor.

The commissioner Taylor ordered the Sikh Army to search each and every Muslim house and arrest who soever was found. Whole night between on 3rd and 4th July, 1857, the Sikh army unleashed the terror in Patna killed the Muslims indiscriminately who soever came in their way. All Ghats of Ganga, Dhobi Ghat, Madarsa Ghat, Chamni Ghat and Tehri Ghat and all other Ghats of Azeemabad were sealed so that no one was able to escape beyond Ganga. Deputy Collector Maula Baksh and Daroghah Nihal Singh, (Nihal Singh was brought by Taylor after the arrest of Maulvi Medhi patrolling Magistrate) made mass arrest of Muslims and they were hanged indiscriminately on the trees without any trial on the orders of Taylor.

Peer Ali Khan and few of his supporters avoided the arrest throughout the night between 3rd and 4th July, 1857, with the hope against hope to get the help from Danapur which did not reach even in the morning of 4th July 1857. Danapur Sepoys could revolt only on 25th July, 1857, i.e. 22 days later.

Before Dawn on 4th morning Peer Ali Khan, Ausaf Ali, Ghulam Abbas and 33 others were arrested. Most of the people arrested were hanged by orders of Taylor on 05.07.1857 itself without any trial. Saiyed Lootf Ali was also arrested in the night of 5th July, 1857. Taylor wanted Peer Ali Khan along with Lootf Ali Khan to be hanged on 5th July, 1857 itself. But General Lloyel and Major Rettery advised him to keep them for few days and interrogate them to extract the information of the conspiracy in detail hence their hanging was deferred. In fact, it was a ploy of Rattery and Farquharson to gain time so that the case of Saiyed Lootf Ali is taken out of Taylor's jurisdiction. Peer Ali Khan's shop was broken open, searched and documents seized. Between 4th July, 1857 to 7th July, 1857 Peer Ali Khan was tortured to get details of all those who were associated with him and his exact antecedents and his association and link with Lootf Ali. But the Shaheed-e-Watan the brave son of village Mohammedpur Maulana Peer Ali Khan did not open his month even on the lurement by Taylor to spare his life if he gives the full details of his associates which according to Taylor included Saiyed Lootf Ali Khan. Peer Ali Khan was produced before Taylor, General Lloyd and Major Rettery the so-called Court on 6th July, 1857 and as pre-determined Peer Ali Khan was sentenced to be hanged till death. Seeing this Mir Abdullah acted fast and got transferred the case of Lootf Ali Khan to the Court of Mr. R.N. Farquharson, a person of his choice as session judge. Seeing this Taylor immediately got Peer Ali hanged on 7th July, 1857. Mir Abdullah used his wealth and relations to save his son, and not only succeeded in saving Lootf Ali but got Taylor removed from the post of Commissioner with disgrace. To save Saiyed Lootf Ali it was necessary that all proofs linking Peer Ali Khan to Lootf Ali and Mir Abdullah remained buried hence enquiries about Peer Ali's antecedents and supporters was stopped. Since Peer Ali was already hanged the case file about him seem to have been closed. This way Saiyed Lootf Ali Khan and the village Mohammedpur as well as the family of Peer Ali Khan escaped the total disaster.

Mufti Intezammullah Shahbai in his book, "Mushaheer-e-Jung Azadi" 1857 to 1956, p. 194, published by Mohd. Saeed and Sons, Karachi (on the reference from book, "Tareekhe Baghawate

Hind", p. 761) says that Peer Ali Khan alongwith his 36 followers which included Saiyed Lootf Ali Khan were arrested and all were hanged except Lootf Ali Khan whose wealth saved him from the gallows.

Shad Azeemabadi writes, p. 74 of his book "Peer Ali":

That Taylor asked Peer Ali before hanging:

Agar tum asal hall se ittela kar do to tumhari jan Bakshi ho. (If you disclose the truth of your movements, your life will be spared).

Peer Ali ne jawab diya:

Raaz ki baten qabile zikr naheen hoteen hain, jo shaksh afsha-e raaz kare who gunahgar hota hai.

(Secrets are not to be disclosed, any one disclosing secrets is punished by ALLAH).

Thomas Rettrey who actually arrested Per Ali Khan narrated the last moments of Peer Ali's hanging as follows:

"Peer Ali the man created considerable trouble to the police in apprehending this ruffian, and had to wound him twice before they succeeded in capturing him. He was a strong, muscular, bull-necked villain with a most villainous, Jack Sheppard", expression of countenance."

On being condemned to death, and being asked if he had anything to say in his defence, he curtly replied that he has and said: "You asked me if I had anything to say, I have:

DO YOU THINK I AM AFRAID TO DIE? NOT. You ask me why I rebelled; I will tell you; you took away our arms, a man would rather give up his life than his arms; you ordered us not to leave our houses after 9:00 am; we are men not children to be sent to bed early. I am a scholar and like to go amongst my friends at night and read with them; one night I was out and met one of your Burkandazes. He asked me why I was out as it was past 9 O'clock. I said friend, I have no watch. He ordered me to return home, which I declined to do; he struck me with a slipper and called up some other Burkandazes took me to the Thana where I was kept all night. The Daroghah released me in the morning and I went home, vowing to be revenged on you Commission who issued there orders; you may hang me, you may hang thousand but that won't make them love you more. The day is *nigh* (near), thank God, when you Feringhees will be out of the Country. Now hang me, I have nothing more to say."

(Ref.: 45th Rattray Sikhs in Delhi, 1886)

The above was a story by Peer Ali to keep Taylor off the track instead giving him the correct details of the people involved in the revolt.

Taylor himself described Peer Ali Khan in his letter dated 08.07.1857 written to the Governor as under:

> "He was cool and defiant to the last, though manacled and wounded, and with the sentence over him, he showed neither fear, nervousness, nor shame. In character, appearance and manners, he was the perfect ideal of a brutal and brave fanatic."

Taylor further quoted to the Governor in his letter dated 08.07.1857 the words of Peer Ali Khan on Taylor's offer of Pordern in case Peer Ali Khan gives full details of his movement, Peer Ali replied:

> "There are some occasions on which it is good to give up life and that, if I, sacrificed, thousand others, everyday, would fill their place."

Charles Allen quotes Taylor's recording to the last words of Peer Ali Khan just before hanging, p. 145:

> "Shortly before his execution Peer Ali was taken before Taylor to be questioned further."
>
> "He was calm, self-possessed and almost dignified. He taunted me with the oppression I had exercised, and concluded his speech by saying –you may hang me, or such as me, everyday, but thousands will rise in my place, and your object will never be gained."

Shad Azeemabadi narrated the last moments of Peer Ali Khan's hanging as under:

> *"Yeh kehta huwa woh darorasan ki azmaish mein kamyab ho gaya aur aaj se sau saal pahle usne Hindustan ki azaadi ke liye pehli qurbani awam ki taraf se pesh kardi."*

Shad Azeemabadi further narrated the last moments of Peer Ali Khan on Gallows:

"Peer Ali hansta hua phansi ke takhte per charh gaya.

(Peer Ali with smile on his face stood on the gallows)

Commissioner uske isteqlal Ko dekh kar aab-aab ho gaya"

(The Commissioner was ashamed to see his cool and confident posture of defiance)

Shad Azeemabadi further writes:

"Aaj uski koi nishani baqui naheen hain magar uski yaad har saal

(He did not leave any of his marks but he is remembered by those

jashne azadi ke manane walon ke dilon me aa jati hai."
(celebrating independence of the country every year.)

Here Shad was mistaken rather ignorant when he wrote that: *uski koi nishani baqui naheen hai* (he did not leave any mark). The Independent India is his *Nishani* (*Mark*). Besides the Independent India, his house, his village (Mohammedpur), his family, and his small landed property which he could have inherited from his father late Mehar Ali Khan, which was inherited by his elder brother Nasrullah Khan and later Nasrullah Khan's future generations which still exists in the village Mohammedpur, Tehsil Nizamabad, Distt. Azamgarh, all are his *Nishanees* (Marks).

Shad is further mistaken when he says that:

> *"Uski yaad har sal jahsne azadi mananey walon ke dilon mein aa jati hai.* (He is remembered every year by those celebrating the independence of the country.)"

No one remembers such selfless martyrs. Here I quote from the news item published in *Quami Awaz*, Urdu Daily dated 17.08.06:

> *Phir Nazar Andaz Kiye Gae Shaheed Peer Ali*
>
> (Again Shaheed Peer Ali Khan is ignored)
>
> *Har Saal Ki Tareh is saal bhi elaqua ke mashoor mujahid-e-aazadi, Shaheed Peer Ali Khan ko Hukoomat Aur intezamia-ne-nazar andaaz kar diya.*
>
> *(Patna, 16 August, S.N.B.)*

As per past years, this year also, the Government and the administration, ignored the famous Mujahid-e-Azaadi, Shaheed Peer Ali.

The 1857, rebellion was by Muslims only, throughout India. The following details of Delhi also proves the same point:

Charles Allen, p. 158 mentions:

> "One rebel Moinuddin Hasan Khan (in Delhi) recorded, 'The green as well as dry trees were consumed, the guiltless shared the same fate as the (so-called) guilty.' As innocent Christans fell victims on the 11th of May, so the same evil fate befell the Mohammedans on the 20th September, 1857. The gallows slew those who had escaped the Sword."

Further, p. 161, it is mentioned:

> "By the end of September, 1857, Delhi was a ghost town entirely cleaned of Muslims, who were increasingly viewed by the Britishers the real enemy. A British officer wrote in a letter to his home in England, 'there has been nothing but shooting these *villains* (Muslims) for the last three days. Some 300 to 400 were shot yesterday.' Areas of the City believed to have given aid and *succor* to the rebels were flattened, including several Mosques. Even the City's great Jamma Masjid was threatened with demolition. For a time it served as a barracks for SIKH troops, and two

years passed before it was finally released to a body of Muslim trustees."

Lacs of Muslim from common men throughout India sacrificed their lives, their family, their properties and gave their blood to the Watne Azeem, Hindustan purely on "Nationalism" still they are called anti-national. Urdu poet Basheer Badar righty said:-

"Khoon Ki quisten to kai de chuke lekin
(Many installments of blood already given, still)

Ai khake watan qarz ada qyun nahee hota."
(O! motherland, why the debts are not clear.)

As against the above the fight of non-Muslims such as Nana and Babu Kunwar Singh even Maharani Lakshmi Bai was because for considerations and reasons other than Nationalism. Still Indian historians described them as great patriots. They are projected as Hero in many school textbooks. No problem. Because these people did fight the Britishers describe them fighters of freedom, but why the sacrifices of Muslims are not projected accordingly. These Muslims did not have any, personal grudge or intended to have anything for personal gain. Why their deeds have been suppressed and put under thick layers of Archives?

The Peer Ali's movement was deep routed. He took the support of even low caste Hindus. But due to preponment of the plan his scheme to make sudden attack with the Danapur Sepoys as well as the Rajwar community of Sukerpore, Barhat and Govindpur around Rajgir could not be co-coordinated. However, few days after the arrest and execution of Peer Ali Khan and his followers the Danapur sepoys as well as the Rajwars revolted.

A.K. Biswas describes the event in his book, "Unsung Martyrs of 1857," Abridged I.K. Shukla:

"Rajwars had raised the banner of revolt against the British empire under the spirited leadership of Jawahir Rajwar, Etwa Rajwar, etc. The Brits were baffled by the guerilla tactics of the Rajwars against which their army felt ineffectual and helpless. The Dy. Major informed the DM Alonzo Money that 'the band of men under Jawahir

Rajwar near Manjhi Nadeergunj have all left and fled into the Rajgir jungle. Another leader Etwa Rajwar had also fled into the hill near Govindpore.' In September, 1857, Worsely disclosed that Etwa and two bands—Murraee and Kurumpore, who were moving armed. The force under Etwa comprised "50 matchlock men and some of the discharged sepoys..... I have also heard that the Zamindars of Mauza Sautaur have aided the rebels Jawahir Rajwar of Mauza Hureepore by furnishing them both with money and supplies and I have heard the badmashes did not plunder their villages. Rendered desperate by their failure in nabbing the rebellious Rajwars, the British resorted to the most dastardly act, open only to cowards and violating norms of civilized behaviour and legality. Worsely visited the villages and wrote to the DM on 22 July, 1858: as none but severe measures will keep the Rajwars in check, and hunting them down in the hills and jungles which they invariably take to would be next to impossible, I suggest that the whole Rajwars in the three above mentioned villages be razed to the ground and their property (if there be any) confiscated to the Government. Such an example may frighten other villages." The imperial terrorism did not spare even women, children, old and infirm. This was the policy laid down by Tayler nearly a year ago.

By 31 July, 1857, Shahabad district was roiling. The Commissioner declared: "matters have now arrived at a crisis at which all considerations yield to the one great object, viz., the prompt re-occupation of Shahabad, the arrest and execution of *Kooer* (Kunwar) Singh, and the infliction of terrible vengeance on the rebellious villagers of that district who have joined in the revolt."

The brutal reprisals suffered by the patriotic Rajwars of Sukerpur, Barhat and Govindpur in common with Peer Ali and his cohorts, are glowing examples of heroic men who withstood the fury of the Empire in our First War of Independence. Now, forgotten, they have become faceless, nameless. Their sacrifices form a memorable chapter of the freedom struggle in Bihar in the 19th century. Their brilliant contribution to our pride as a nation remains eclipsed in the archives. Rajwars in Bihar even today are treated contemptuously.

The first systematic census of 1871 called them semi-Hinduised aboriginal numbering 53,000, who swelled to 132,000 in 1911, and 237,370 in 1981. Their anti-imperialist struggles during the Revolt of Hindustan did not make them socially respectable, nor was it at all deemed worthy of record or notice in history. Socially ostracized, they were forever dogged by degradation and destitution. No good Brahman ever served them as family priest. The ten-fold indicators of social status or stigma for a Hindu were enunciated by the Census Commissioner E.A. Gait, ICS, in 1911. One was the Brahmanical yardstick—whether a person is served by a good Brahmin as a family priest. It was regarded an indicator of social dignity. Otherwise, one would be held in low esteem. In post-colonial India Rajwar is a Scheduled Caste in Bihar. They never received the benefit of education in the 50 years of "freedom". They are as ignored and exploited now as in Brit India.

And, those loyal to the Crown were sumptuously rewarded. Who were they? Upper caste, upper class predators and parasites. The DM, Gaya, received a delegation on Ist August, 1857 of Gayawal Brahmins who offered to supply, in concert with the Zamindars, 3000-4000 men to fight against the freedom fighters. This development was avidly reported the same day by DM Alonzo Money to A.R. Young, Secy. to Government in Calcutta.The feudal lords—Zamindars, Talookdars, Thikadars and even the intelligentsia, with no shame or embarrassment, flaunted their loyalty to the beastly British aliens. Arrayed against their country and fellow nationals.

The Gayawals were the custodians of Gaya shrines, a center of pilgrimage for the Hindus offering *pind dan* to their dead ancestors. Gaya was close to Rajgir where

Rajwars had risen in revolt. The British could not conceal their glee. This was the elitist treason that has marked the upper classes and upper castes ever since. In post-colonial India the British rule is identified with subjugation of Indian aspiration, exploitation, and tyranny. But the Gayawals had no compunction in siding with the enemy. Those holy men of Gaya redefined the meaning of treason (and thought it patriotism to sell the nation to foreigners, just like today).

To cite another example, Raghunandan Singh, the Maharaja of Darbhanga, offered rewards of Rs. 30 to anyone capturing an army deserter or a mutinous sepoy! His gesture was loudly cheered by the beleaguered British and duly reciprocated with conspicuous marks of imperial favour. But these were not solitary or stray instances. There were many others—influential, powerful and reputed–in various walks of life, who financially and materially supported the British—the foreign invaders. They haven't suffered any stigma in pubic or official dispensation. Many hogged encomiums and limelight for their "unique contributions and sacrifices to the cause of national freedom," when India celebrated her 50th Anniversary of Independence!

"The nation that substitutes its patriots with traitors, that denigrates its heroes, and anoints slaveowners, remains enslaved".

I further quote, Sir Henry Himiltan Thoms and Lord Ellenborough the Governor-General (1842 AD) about the role of Muslims and Hindus in the Independence Movement India in 18th and 19th centuries.

Sir Henry Himilton Thoms:

"I have already stated earlier that the real originator of revolt of 1857, were not Hindus. Now I am trying to show that this revolt was the result of Muslim conspiracy. If Hindus are restricted to their choice and wishes they will never participate in any such conspiracy nor they were willing to do so."

Lord Ellenborough:

"I am fully convinced that those special individual who are surviving on our *dole* (Tukdon per) were against our interest. As against that Hindus were celebrating our victory. When we are sure of Muslims enmity with us who are 1:10 only, then why not we support those who are 9:1 and are our loyal."

He further writes:

" How can I close my eyes to the truth that this generation of Muslims are our enemy to the extent of madness, hence for this our policy should be shown our goodness to Hindus."

(Ref.: "Tehreek-e-Azadi men Ullema Ka Kirdar", pp. 52-53).

13

Reasons for Failure of the 1857 Revolt and Role of Sir Saiyed Ahmad Khan and His Loyalty to Britishers

During the 1857, movement there were many groups and each were concerned and motivated on different grounds. The country was not one country in modern sense, but collection of various areas inhabited by diverse groups with autonomous local chief.

The Britishers one-after-the-other captured, the States of various rulers, by treachery, treason, fraud and force. Out of such Native rulers, only Sirajuddula, Teepu Sultan, Nana Rao, Rani Lakshmi Bai and Begham Hazrat Mahal faught to save their ruled territory or for the grudge they had against the Britishers of having deprived their elders or them from the ownership of the respective territory. It was not at all fight for any national cause. No such concept existed at that time. Out of all the above named rulers only Teepu Sultan had the vision of nationalism and made efforts to remove the Britishers from Indian Soil and for this purpose he made efforts to unite all the big or small rulers of the country in the cause of removing not only Britishers but all the Europeans from Indian Soil. He declared and only he declared "India for Indians" and not for Teepu Sultan nor he ever intended to capture entire India from the hands of other rulers. Brief details about Nana Rao and Maharani Lakshmi Bai is given ahead which will show their reason to fight Britishers. Only because Nana Rao and Maharani Lakshmi Bai faught with Britishers, the historians specially Indian historians brought them to the bracket of "Freedom Fighters" one may accept it. But the projection of Teepu Sultan as the communal, anti-Hindu ruler is a great injustice to him. His fight was purely a Nationalist movement.

Besides the above rulers, there were some individuals, such as General Bakt Khan, General Mehmood Khan, Khan Bahadur Khan, Tantia Tope, Shehzada Firoze Shah, Mohammed Khan of Bijnore, Abdurrehman of Jhajjar, Hasan Ali Khan of Dojana, (he was former Governor of Gorakhpur and lost his post after the annexation of Oudh), Nahar Singh of Ballabhgarh, Tularam of Rewari, Walidad Khan of Malagarh, Ahmad Ali Khan of Farrukhanagar, Mehdi Hasan of Sultanpur, Fazle Azim of Rai Bareili, Banda Hussain a Lft. of Mehdi Hasan, Rao Sahib, Maulvi Sarfaraz Ali of Gorakhpur Maulvi Sikandar Shah of Faizabad, Ghaus Mohd. Khan of Sikandar Rao and Brigadier Jwala Prasad, (hanged near Chausa Ghat on 03.05.1860) were generals and were ready and willing to associates with the rulers if they wanted to fight the Britishers but could do nothing because the Local rulers did not unite against the British hence most of them died and became Martyrs. Their 1st and foremost object of fight was nothing but removal of Britishers from Indian Soil and not to capture any Territory as their dominion. These people were nationalist in the sense that they faught only in the area they belonged. Teepu Sultan's consideration was only to save the honour of India, and India has to be saved from being enslaved by British. Unfortunately no Indian ruler realised their national duty to respond positively to the call of Teepu rather most of them sided with the Britishers. These Generals, Mujahide Azaadi would have supported the efforts of Teepu Sultan and others if Teepu's call for "Jehad" for cleaning the dirty designs of British would have been positively responded by other rulers of the country.

Then there was another group comprising of Ulema (Call them Wahabee's or by any name) but they called upon the common men to get ready for "Jehad-e-Azadi-ea-Hindustan." Prominent of them, Maulvi Ahmadullah Madarasi alongwith Maulvi Massih-us-Zaman and Babar Ali in Oudh Maulvi Liyaqat Ali in Allahabad and Maulvi Peer Ali Khan in Patna division were working and generating public opinion against the Britishers. They were the people who did not have any personal ambitions nor were greedy of power for themselves but only "National" objective. They were neither terrorist nor fanatic but even if one may want to call them as such as the Britishers and British historians call them, I say, I am proud of such so-called terrorist/ fanatics who attained Martyrdom for the Azadi of the Motherland Hindustan.

There sacrifices are buried under the thick layers of Archives and our historians feel shy to write about them and their sacrifices because most of them are Muslims and that Hindus did not support them rather supported the Britishers.

Sir Saiyed Ahmad Khan who was in Bijnore during the uprising of 1857 has tried to condemn the Maulvis who participated or worked against Britishers.

Sir Saiyed Ahmad Khan, has been described by the Columnist Hamid Hussain, "As a child he (Saiyed Ahmad) sat at the lap of Major General David Ochterlony, the British resident in Delhi and played with the gold buttons of his uniform. His maternal grand father (Nana), Khwaja Farid-ud-Din, who left early childhood impression on Saiyed Ahmad had served the British in several important assignments. Saiyed had accepted the permanent status of power of British in India and considered the attempts to subvert the authority of British, a challenge to the legitimate authority. He was posted in April 1858 as Principal Sadar-e-Amin in Moradabad by the British Government Saiyed Ahmad being present in person during 1857 in Western U.P. his narrations may help to know the detailed events of the time but cannot be used for comprehensive analysis due to obvious his bias in favour of British."

Hamid Hussain further said:

> "Similarly Vinayak Damodar Sawarkar published his works in 1909 with the title 'History of the War of Independence.' But his work was more of imposing one's ideological bent, on a historical situation."

Sawarkar a declared anti-Muslim and preacher of Hindutva was not expected to write the great deeds of Muslims, moreover, he wrote in 1909 when British were at their peak of control of the country and he wanted to prove his loyalty to British.

As for Sir Saiyed Ahmad there is no doubt that he was absolutely pro-britisher but he had the urge for the good of Muslim community. He found that because of the abolition of Persian as Court language large number of Muslims became unemployed. English Magistrates replaced Muslim who were attached in the Courts as Qazis or Muftees. Hindus immediately adopted the English language thus not only retained their already existing positions in revenue departments which they held from the time of Muslims rule but also captured the posts in other departments. As for Muslims were concerned they were being advised by then Ulema not to learn English and not to go to the schools started by Britishers. Sir Saiyed Ahmad Khan must have also became concerned with the situation arising out of an advertisement published in a Persian Newspaper dated 16th July, 1857 and in the officials Guzzet issued by the Office of the Commissioner of Sunder Ban that there were few vacancies in the office concerned but the vacancies will be filled by only Hindus and no one. Alarmed with such situations Sir Saiyed Ahmad Khan must have taken upon himself the cause of Muslims but in this effort he exceeded the limit. In doing so he condemned the Ulema as imposters. He tried his best to bring Muslim masses to study English so that their unemployment position could be checked. He could have achieved the same object by having restrained approach on his utterances and writings against those Muslims and Ulema who were fighting against the Britishers. Allama Shibli Naumani of Azamgarh is the example of the same period. He also advocated to the Muslims to learn English and for this purpose established a School which is today a post-graduate college. He did not condemn the Muslims who were opposed to Britishers, as Sir Saiyed did Allama Shibli achieved the same objective without self-condemnation.

14

The Role of Nana Rao, Maharani Lakshmi Bai, Tantia Tope and their Ultimate End

The reasons of Nana Rao and Rani Lakshmi Bai to fight Britishers are described by G.W. Forrest (Vol. I, pp. 403-07, 420) are as under:

Nana Rao

"The Nana Rao's full name was 'Teerek Dhunder Pant'. He was born at a small hamlet at the foot of the Ghauts (Ghat) thirty miles east of Bombay, he was adopted by Baji Rao II, the seventh and the last of the Brahmin Peshwas or Mysore of the Palace, who were the real heads of the great Maratha's confederacy. Baji Rao-II was defeated by British at the battle of Kirkee (30th October, 1817) his forts were taken and he himself surrendered on the assurance by Britishers that 'Baji Rao-II shall receive a liberal pension from the company's Government for the support of himself and family. The amount of this pension will be fixed by the Governor-General; but Brigadier-General Malcolm takes upon himself to engage that it shall not be less than eight lakhs of rupees per annum.' Lord Hastings, the Governor-General was annoyed of the terms but honoured them. A proclamation having been issued before surrender 'that his dominions had been forfeited, and that the Peshwa and his family were forever excluded from the throne" Baji Rao and his family were conducted to Bithor, a small town twelve miles up the river from Cawnpore. Here he lived and at his death in 1851 he left all his property, amounting to £ 2,80,000 to his adopted son Dhunder Pant. (Though the widows of Peshawa Baji Rao-II disputed the will as forged one). However, the annual sum of Rs. 8,00,000 paid to Baji Rao was decided by East India Company as the grant only till the life of Baji Rao-II ceased on his death.

Nana appealed to the Government at England against the decision of the East India Company India and dispatched his confidential man, Azeemullah Khan but his mission failed."

At the footnote, p. 405, G.W. Forrest quotes Captain Mawbray Thonson about Azimoolah:

"Azimoolah was originally a 'Khitmatgar' (waiter at table) in some Anglo-Indian family: profiting by the opportunity thus afforded to him, he acquired a thorough acquaintance with the English and French languages both spoken and written. He subsequently were a teacher, in a Cawnpore Government School, and then was subjected to become the Vakeel or prime agent of the Nana. And was deputed by Nana to England to press upon the authorities in leaden-hall street the application for the continuance of Baji Rao's pension. He reached London in the season of 1854."

On return he stayed at Constantinople just after the repulse of the Allies, on 18th June, 1854. He said that he crossed over to Crimea in order to see, 'those great Roostums, the Russions, who have beaten French and English together.'

"Failure in his attempt to have the pension was the chief cause of the grudge which the Nana owed against England. It was natural enough that Nana should hate Britishers who compelled his adopted father to perpetual banishment. Dhunder Pant a Maratha endowed with strong social and religious prejudices and aspirations of the mountaineer who had struck the last blow for Hindu supremacy. The power of the English he had been told

> by Azimoolah, his trusted agent, had begun to Wane, and it would be strange if he did not think the time was opportune for striking another blow for Hindu Supremacy."

Tantia Tope after his capture by Britishers in his as well as his brother Nana stated:

> "Nana acted under compulsion." "The sepoys of 3 regiments of infantry and the 2nd light cavalry surrounded us, and imprisoned the Nana and myself in the treasury and plundered the magazines and treasury. They told Nana, Maharaja a kingdom awaits you, if you join our cause, but death if you side with our enemies."

Rani Laksmi Bai

W.G. Forrest in his book "A History of Indian Mutiny", p. 182 Vol-III, describes the events which made Lakshmi Bai revolt against British.

> "In 1817, the Peshawa ceded the State of Jhansi to the British, and its new ruler acknowledged, the hereditary title of the local ruler, and fifteen years later i.e. in 1832 advanced him to the dignity of Rajah."

In 1835, the "Raja" died, after having adopted a son. The British Government refused to recognize the adopted son and selected a great uncle of the Raja to succeed. Three years later he also died childless. The British Government selected the brother of the declared Rajah to be his successor. He ruled for eleven years but died with no son, but just before death from the death bed in 1853 he adopted a son. But the British Government of East India Company refused to recognize the adopted son as the legal successor and Jhansi was annexed to East India Company's direct rule.

In Northern Western provinces, British had adopted the policy of not resuming the Jagirs after the death of the holder to its descendents. Instead they gave the heirs fixed pension. Even this pension was being denied if the recipient of the pension did not have a direct descendant male child. In this way between 1847-56, the East India Company swallowed, Nagpur, Jhansi, Satara, Sambhalpore and denied the pension to Nana and many others.

G.B. Malleson, p. 32, writes:

> "With a stroke of pen converted the lady so high in spirit and character into a veritable tigress against English. Rani of Jhansi hated English with all the bitterness of a woman, regarded herself as having been grievously wronged. The high-spirited woman was deprived of the right which she believed to her legal and legitimate rights. She was highly gifted possessed great energy, a high character being much respected by everyone in Jhansi."

The widow of the late Rajah, the Ranee (The Rani Lakshmi Bai) was offered a pension of £ 6,000 a year which she first refused it, as pittance but later accepted it. The Rani Lakshmi Bai was tall in stature, handsome (G.W. Forrest used the word handsome for her hence I am also referring her as such) in person, young energetic, proud and unyielding, and from that moment indulged the stern passions of anger and revenge.

On 1st June, 1857, 12th Regiment of Native infantry, raised the standard of revolt, followed by other native regiments. Captain Gordon sent urgent message to Rani for help but she refused on the ground that she has been threatened to be killed by the mutineers if she accepts the request of Captain Gordon.

The Rani remained indifferent to the revolt, neither helped Britishers nor participated in the Revolt. The Mutineer ultimately threatened the Rani with instant death if she refused to throw in her lot with the rebels. She accordingly consented, and supplied then with a re-enforcement of 1000 men, and two heavy guns which she ordered to be dug out of the Earth, which were buried three years ago. The Rani kept on watching the situation, and only in the middle of March 1858, Rani of Jhansi with her handmaids, wrapped in bright, radiant vesture, went to the batteries and roused the zeal of her soldiers by her presence and her fiery words.

Columnist Hamid Husain looks at the 1857 war of Independence with title of "The story of the storm 1857" based on the book "The Sepoy rebellion" by Agha H. Amin mentions:

"Lakshmi Bai, the Rani of Jhansi's role is some what controversial. Although she alongwith several local chief had grievances against British. It has not been proven that she had any role in the Mutiny of 12th BM and 13th irregular cavalry stationed at Jhansi on June 5th. She had to pay ransom to the rebels before they left Jhansi. In fact, on June 12 and 14 she wrote letters to Erskine, the Commissioner of Sagar Division assuring him that she would hold Jhansi on behalf of British. Erskine in a formal letter authorized her to collect the revenue. She led her troops against Dewan of Orchna an old rival. She sided with the British but later due to ambiguous British diplomacy and declining of her protestations of loyalty she decided to fight with British. Thereafter, she personally commanded the defence of Jhansi working with defenders who consisted of mutineers. She not only showed her superior administrative and military skills but also personal bravery in combat. She only trusted the five hundred Kabuli Pathans of her army, who escorted her after her defeat at Jhansi. She earned the respect and praise of her enemies when she died on the battle field at Gwalier."

Karl Marx, book, pp. 197-98:

"June 19, 1858, in the battle at the Lashkar Hill, before Gwalier Maharani Lakshmi Bai of Jhansi was killed. Her army dispersed after much slaughter and Gwalier fell to English hand."

As against such brave posture of Rani Lakshmi Bai how shameful were the Sindhia's, in the words of G.B. Malleson, p. 29:

"In 1844, the house of Sindhia, defeated in battle was at the feet of Lord Ellenborough, (begging) that the noble men impose upon it no penalty."

Sindhias did not display any self or national respect just to save their life and title of Raja a Charity from British.

Babu Kunwar Singh

The financial position of Kunwar Singh was very bad. Mr. G.W. Forrest in his book, p. 431, based on the Official Report dated 3rd August, 1857 of Mr. Wake the Magistrate of Shahabad has mentioned as under:

> "Kunwar Singh, a great landlord of Rajput, descent in the district of Shahabad. In 1856, his creditors became pressing, and he sought the aid of Government. He was treated by the Lt. Governor with marked personal kindness, and a scheme was arranged for the payment of his debts. He had proposed to get a loan of twenty lakhs for this object, and this sum was to be liquidated from the proceeds of his large estates through the collectors of Shahabad. A year passed, but he had not procured the loan, and the Board of Revenue sent him a message through the Commissioner of the Division that unless he obtained the entire sum within a month they would recommend Government to abandon the management of his estates. The Board of Revenue considered they had no alternative between surrendering the management of the estate or obtaining the money which he had engaged to borrow in order to place his affairs on a sound footing. But the Board could not possibly discern the heart of the situation; he could not borrow twenty lakhs to pay his debts, for he could hardly find money enough to pay the interest of them. Though the owner of vast estate, Kunwar Singh was in reality when the mutiny began a ruined man—ruined by his own extravagance. He had lavished money upon his ancestral castle at Jagdishpur near Arrah; he had spent large sums of money in building a vast Hindu temple; he had indulged in the luxury of a law suit which had gone against him. Kunwar Singh was on his beam ends. Mr. Wake, the Magistrate of District Shahabad wrote to the Government on 19th July, 1857 that as long as law and order exists

his position cannot improve, take them away, he would become supreme in the District. Koer Singh felt that a revolution might free him from the entanglement that surrounded him."

"With this object in mind: 'He played his game with great skill. He filled his castle with provisions and munitions of war, and he was profuse in his expressions of loyalty and sympathy. He had the social habits and amiable qualities which win friends.' He was described by one who knew him as 'a fine, noble-looking man, at once dignified and courteous, and bore the stamp of real nobility.' He had been in his younger days 'a great sportsman, and was much liked by Europeans generally'. William Taylor also considered him as such. Mr. Taylor wrote to Government on 14th June, 1857 saying, 'Many people have sent me letters inputting disloyalty and disaffection to several of the Zameendars, specially to Babu Kunwar Singh. My personal friendship for him and the attachment he has always shown me, enable me confidently to contradict the report.' But there were officers in the district who did not express the same belief in the loyalty of Kunwar Singh. Mr. Taylor sent an agent to him to intimate the suspicions entertained of his loyalty and to bid him to repair to Patna. The agent was at the same time directed to scrutinize everything connected with and about Kunwar Singh and to submit a confidential report regarding it to the Commissioner. Taylor had not learnt that dissimilation is a weak policy. Kunwar Singh was not likely to leave his castle and place himself in the power of the Commissioner. He received the agent lying on a bed, and pleaded age and infirmity in reply to the Commissioner's summons, but pledged himself to repair to Patna as soon as his health would permit and the Brahmins could find a propitious day for the journey. The Brahmins never found a propitious day, and the old Rajput Chief let it be known that he would resist if force were attempted. The native agent, in his confidential report, stated it was well-known that they (his people) would follow him as their feudal

Chieftain in the event of his raising the standard of rebellion; but beyond this nothing was ascertained. As soon as he heard of Mutiny at Danapur. Kunwar Singh raised the standard of revolt, and sent a large contingent to join the mutineers at Arrah. The Sepoys repeatedly declared they were acting under his express orders; and after a short time he was seen on the parade, and remained during the siege."

At p. 122, "God's Terrorists" Allen writes:

"Raja Kunwar Singh had become so debt ridden that the Bengal Government Board of revenue had stepped into manage his affairs on behalf of his creditors. Early in 1857, Halliday ordered the Board of Revenue to stop bailing out Kunwar Singh, effectively ruining him. Upto this point Kunwar Singh had been a good friend to Bill Taylor and, for all his troubles, had always professed his loyalty to the British Raj. Taylor protested to Halliday about this action against Kunwar Singh threatening that this may alienate Kunwar Singh and his many fellow Rajputs in the region."

I leave the readers to judge for themselves if Peer Ali Khan could have depended on Kunwar Singh's support or was Kunwar Singh dependable to be relied upon.

The above are the historians' description of the cause and reasons of Nana Rao, Rani Lakshmi Bai and Babu Kunwar Singh. I leave the people to judge themselves, whether the sacrifices of Nana Rao or Maharani Lakshmi Bai, who did fight the Britishers very bravely but did they fight for National Cause? As against that I leave for the people to judge, was not the sacrifices of persons such as Saiyed Ahmad Shaheed (being described and equated as Osama Bin Laden of 18th century), Maulvi Ahmadullah Madrasi, Maulvi Liyaqat Ali, Maulvi Peer Ali Khan and such others; purely on National cause? Why our historians have not included them as National heroes and Shaheed-e-Watan? Even now after 150 years no one remembers them. Do not you think great injustice has been done to them?

The Poet Umar Nehtori has rightly said:

"Zalim Ki Buzdilon Ne Ata-ut Qubool Kee
(The Cowards accepted the authority of the Tyrants)

Lekin Mujahidon Ne Shahadat Qubool Kee"
(But the "Mujahids" accepted the Martyrdom instead)

Bibliography

Our Crisis or Three Months at Patna During the Insurrection of 1857 by William Taylor, published by Thaeker, Spinic and Co. Calcutta in 1858.

Thirty-eight Years in India (English), Vol. II By William Taylor, published by W.H. Allen & Co. London, 1882.

Memoirs of William Taylor an Abridged Edition (English) By Chaturbhuj published by Mittal Publications, New Delhi in 1990 from the original book "38 Years in India" in 2 Vols, by William Taylor published in England in 1881-82.

Peer Ali (Urdu) by Jamal Shad Azeemabadi published by Maktaba Jamia, New Delhi.

A History of Indian Mutiny (English) by T.R.E. Holms, 5th Edition published by Mc-Millan and Co. Ltd., St. Martins Street-London, 5th Edition, 1913 (1st Ed., 1897).

A History of Indian Mutiny (English) by G.W. Forrest Reprint by Gautam Jetly for Asian Educational Services, 31, Hauze Khass Village, New Delhi in 3 Vols in 2006 original published by William Black Wood & Sons Edinbarg, London in 1904.

The First War of Independence 1857-59 (English) by Karl Marx and F. Engels published by Foreign Languages Publishing House, Moscow based on the Russian Edition prepared by the Institute of Marxism-Leninism of the C.C.C.P.U. in 1959.

Tareekh-e-Azadi-Men Ulemas Ka Kirdar (before 1857) (Urdu) by Faisal Ahmed Bhatkali Nadvi-Published by Majlise Tehqeeqat Wa Nashriat Islam Lucknow, 1st Edition June, 2003.

History of Aurangzeb, Vol. 5 (English) by Sir Jadavnath Sarkar Kt. C.I.E. Honorary Member, Royal Asiatic Society of Great Britain, Published by Oriental Longman Ltd., Calcutta.

Bagi-e-Hindustan (Urdu) by Mohd. Abdul Shahid Khan Sherwani based on the writing of Allama Fazle-Haque Khairabadi during his exile in Andaman and Nikobar Island, published by Al-Jameh Islam Faizul Uloon, Mohammadabad Azamgarh, U.P. 4th Edition in 1946.

Kashi-Ka-Itihaas, 1st Edition (Hindi) by Dr. Moti Chand, published by Hindi Garanth Ratnakar P. Ltd., Heerabagh, Bombay in 1962.

Indian Mutiny (English) by G.B. Malleson: Reprint by Gautam Jetly 6A Shahpur Jat, New Delhi, Original published in London in 1894.

Advance History of Medival India (English) by J.L. Mehta Publisher: Sterling Publishes P. Ltd., New Delhi, 1979.

Last Moghal (English) by William Dalrymple published by Penguin, New Delhi, London in 2006.

God's Terrorist (English) by Charles Allen published by Little Brown London in 2006.

Karwan-e-Rafta (Urdu) by Naqui Ahmed Irshad, published by Khuda Bhakhsh Oriental Public Library, Patna in 1995.

Salateen-e-Hind (Urdu) Vols. 1 and 2 by Hakeem Mufti Intezamullah Saheb Shenbai Akbarabadi, published by Nadvatul Musannafeen Urdu Bazar, Delhi, 1966-67.

Tehreek-e-Azaadi (Urdu) by Maulana Abbul Kalam Azaad, publishsed by Shaheed Book Centre, 9/5539, Purana Saleempur, Delhi–31 in 1986.

Mushaheer-e-Jung-e-Azadi (Urdu) published by Mohd. Saeed and Sons, Karachi.

Maqalate Tarikh-e-Hind (Urdu) published by Khudabaksh Oriental Public Library-Patna, 2001.

Hindustan Times (English), New Delhi, dated 30.08.2006 and dated 19.11.2006.

Rashtriya Shahara (Urdu), Dated 14.08.2005

National Herald, New Delhi, Dated 21.10.2006 article by Dr. B.M. Sankhdhar.

Qaumi Awaz Daily (Urdu), Dated 17.08.2006 and 24.01.2007.

Delhi Mid-Day (English), Dated 12.08.2005.

Unsung Martyrs of 1857 by A.K. Biswas abridged by I.K. Shukla.

Index